www.wadsworth.com

www.wadsworth.com is the World Wide Web site for
Thomson Wadsworth and is your direct source to dozens
of online resources.

At *www.wadsworth.com* you can find out about supple-
ments, demonstration software, and student resources. You
can also send email to many of our authors and preview
new publications and exciting new technologies.

www.wadsworth.com
Changing the way the world learns®

Guide to Criminal Law
for New York

Guide to Criminal Law
for New York

Second Edition

TIM BAKKEN
Department of Law
United States Military Academy at West Point

MARGARET STOCK
Department of Law
United States Military Academy at West Point

MARK WELTON
Department of Law
United States Military Academy at West Point

THOMSON

WADSWORTH

Australia • Canada • Mexico • Singapore • Spain • United Kingdom • United States

Executive Editor: Sabra Horne
Development Editor: Julie Sakaue
Assistant Editor: Jana Davis
Editorial Assistant: Elise Smith
Marketing Manager: Terra Schultz
Marketing Assistant: Annabelle Yang

Project Manager, Editorial Production: Jennifer Klos
Print Buyer: Emma Claydon
Permissions Editor: Kiely Sexton
Cover Designer: Yvo Riezebos
Cover Image: Donovan Reese/Getty Images
Text and Cover Printer: Thomson West

For more information about our products,
contact us at:
Thomson Learning Academic Resource Center
1-800-423-0563

For permission to use material from this text or product,
submit a request online at
http://www.thomsonrights.com.

Any additional questions about permissions
can be submitted by email to
thomsonrights@thomson.com.

Library of Congress Control Number: 2004109558

ISBN: 0-534-64417-1

Thomson Wadsworth
10 Davis Drive
Belmont, CA 94002-3098
USA

Asia
Thomson Learning
5 Shenton Way #01-01
UIC Building
Singapore 068808

Australia/New Zealand
Thomson Learning
102 Dodds Street
Southbank, Victoria 3006
Australia

Canada
Nelson
1120 Birchmount Road
Toronto, Ontario M1K 5G4
Canada

Europe/Middle East/South Africa
Thomson Learning
High Holborn House
50/51 Bedford Row
London WC1R 4LR
United Kingdom

Latin America
Thomson Learning
Seneca, 53
Colonia Polanco
11560 Mexico D.F.
Mexico

Spain/Portugal
Paraninfo
Calle/Magallanes, 25
28015 Madrid, Spain

Guide to Criminal Law for New York

Contents

Guide to Criminal Law
for New York

Chapter One

The Nature, Origins, and Purposes of Criminal Law

Introduction

In New York, the legislature has created the State's penal code by compiling statutes that make certain conduct or actions punishable by imprisonment, death, or other restraints on liberty, such as probation. The statutes that cover criminal conduct are contained in the "New York Penal Law." These statutes form the basis of New York's substantive criminal law (an adjunct to New York's Criminal Procedure Law). Only the United States and New York Constitutions can limit criminal law and criminal procedure. This book surveys New York's substantive criminal law.

In colonial times and during the first half of the 20th Century, the criminal law in the United States was often determined by community standards, as reflected in judicial decisions, which can be thought of as the "common law." For example, assume that in a prior case a court held that "carnal knowledge" constituted what today is called "forcible rape." In a new case, a prosecutor, based on a perception of community norms, might ask a court to extend the definition of "carnal knowledge to include an adult male who had consensual sexual intercourse with a minor female, an act that today might be called "statutory rape." In essence, the court would interpret contemporary community standards to determine whether a man's sexual intercourse with a girl violated community norms and thus constituted carnal knowledge, a crime created by a judge.

This kind of judicial decision-making can be unfair, however, because it tells society what is right or wrong (that is, what is or is not "criminal") only after an individual has committed a particular action. Thus, such decision-making can violate notions of due process in that individuals are not notified prior to committing an act whether the act is permissible. In such a common law criminal justice system, people may decide not to engage in what may be perfectly proper, productive behavior for fear that a court will later determine their behavior to be "criminal."

As a result, to some extent, all states codified their criminal law in penal codes that were established by state legislatures. Today, the penal codes indicate what behavior is prohibited. If an individual is contemplating a certain action, such as a complicated financial transaction, the person can look to the state (and federal) penal codes prior to engaging in financial transactions and so determine whether the contemplated transactions are legal, and thus not "criminal."

In New York, the legislature calls the state penal code the "Penal Law" (New York Penal Law 1.00). The purpose of the Penal Law in New York is to: (1) indicate what conduct is prohibited; (2) give fair warning that the conduct is prohibited; (3) define the prohibited conduct; (4) differentiate between serious (felony) and less serious (misdemeanor) crimes; (5) provide appropriate penalties; and (6) insure public safety and deterrence of crime and rehabilitation of offenders (New York Penal Law 1.05).

1

Three important goals of New York's criminal law, as stated in the Penal Law, are to insure public safety, deterrence of crime, and rehabilitation of offenders. It is the responsibility of the New York courts to interpret and apply the Penal Law in criminal cases. In the following case, the court was required to decide whether all three of these goals must be considered when sentencing an individual who has been convicted of a crime.

[The case opinions contained in this book (including the paragraphs, sentences, and citations) have been significantly edited. For a complete version of the cases, please find the case reporters (the books that contain the cases) by using the citations included at the beginning of every case. All cases are from the New York Court of Appeals, New York's highest court, unless noted. If a case has been decided by one of New York's four intermediate appellate courts, there will a note in the parenthesis of every case citation indicating which appellate court decided the case (1st, 2nd, 3rd, or 4th department). The parentheses also contain the year in which the court decided a particular case.]

People v. Burgh, 89 A.D.2d 672, 453 N.Y.S.2d 783 (3rd Department 1982)

Defendant and his accomplice, Grayson Banks, robbed at knifepoint a Binghamton taxi driver. During the robbery the driver received knife wounds to his face and hand. Banks confessed shortly after being arrested. The police investigation which followed revealed that defendant was the other man involved. Each was accused in a one-count indictment of aiding and abetting the other in committing robbery in the first degree. Before trial, Banks pleaded guilty as charged and received a sentence of 3 to 9 years. Defendant, who elected to be tried, was convicted of the same offense and was sentenced to a term of imprisonment of not less than 6 2/3 years and not greater than 20 years.

Defendant contends, among other things, that ... there is no justification for the wide disparity between his sentence and that received by his accomplice, who pleaded guilty to the same offense, and further that in determining defendant's sentence the court failed to give consideration to his potential for rehabilitation. It is not at all clear from the record that defendant's actions were more culpable than those of his accomplice, whose sentence was much lighter; the testimony about who wielded the knife that injured the victim was confused and contradictory and if anything it appeared that Banks played a larger role in wounding the driver. Nor does the record suggest that their criminal histories are so dissimilar as to warrant the breadth of the difference in their sentences. Indeed, the presentence report showed that defendant, an unemployed Korean War veteran, had one prior brush with the law, a charge of criminal trespass and petit larceny for which he received a conditional discharge of one year. Most importantly, the court in sentencing defendant stated: "I'm not concerned with rehabilitation. I'm concerned with the penal aspects of the sentence." Deterrence and retribution are valid sentencing objectives, but so too is a defendant's rehabilitative needs. Rehabilitation is a stated goal of the Penal Law (§ 1.05, subd 5). A sentencing Judge is obliged to give due consideration to the purposes of imprisonment: "Societal protection, rehabilitation and deterrence" (People v Farrar, 52 NY2d 302, 305). Although defendant's rehabilitation is only one factor to be considered, we believe it was error to disregard it entirely. [Judgment modified and, as so modified, affirmed].

In the Burgh case, the Court of Appeals interpreted the Penal Law to require judges to consider rehabilitation in sentencing. In contrast, in recent years many states and the federal government have focused less on rehabilitation and more on incapacitating offenders. In New York, county prosecutors, who are elected District Attorneys, are charged with enforcing the intent of the legislature. District Attorneys initiate almost all criminal cases (in the name of the "People") in lower courts, where the cases are tried. [The New York Attorney General may institute a limited number of criminal prosecutions.] If the prosecutor obtains a conviction, the defendant is then entitled to lodge an appeal in the New York appellate courts. Under the double jeopardy clauses of the United States and New York Constitutions, the prosecutor can never appeal a verdict of "not guilty." Although various courts can exercise jurisdiction over misdemeanor cases (such as the Criminal Court in the five counties of New York City), felony cases in New York are often processed and/or tried in what is called the "County Court" or the "Supreme Court."

If a defendant is convicted, he or she may appeal to one of the four intermediate appellate courts in New York that has jurisdiction over the county where the conviction occurred. Each of the intermediate appellate courts is called the "Supreme Court, Appellate Division." The courts are designated "First Department," "Second Department," "Third Department," and "Fourth Department." Depending on the decisions of the four appellate courts, a defendant or the prosecution may request the right to appeal the decision of the intermediate appellate court to the highest court in New York. The highest court is called the "New York Court of Appeals," which is the equivalent of what most other states designate as their "Supreme Courts."

The Application of the Criminal Law

Ideally, a state legislature should define every action (or lack of action, which is usually termed an "omission") that is criminal prior to the commission of the action so as to provide notice about what are prohibited and required human actions. However, in reality, there are innumerable situations that can arise in life, and it is not possible to contemplate every situation. By nature, then, criminal laws, designated in the Penal Codes as "statutes," must be drafted broadly by the legislature to cover as many prohibited human actions as possible. When there is a question about whether a statute covers a particular action, courts are called upon to determine a statute's applicability. In deciding how or whether a statute applies, courts, such as the Court of Appeals in the case below, often look to the nature, origins, and purpose of a statute.

In the following case, People v. Carroll, the Court of Appeals considers whether the broad language in a statute, Penal Law 260.10(2), covers a stepmother's failure to care for her husband's daughter. That is, is a stepmother a "parent, guardian, or other person" legally responsible for the care of her husband's daughter? In a society that values individualism, consider whether or under what circumstances one person should have responsibility to care for another person.

People v. Carroll, 93 N.Y.2d 564, 715 N.E.2d 500, 693 N.Y.S.2d 498 (1999)

Over the course of several days, three-year-old Shanaya Jones was beaten to death by her father. Defendant, the child's stepmother, witnessed most of the violence, but did not alert the authorities or summon medical assistance until Shanaya was dead. The issue before us is whether the Grand Jury that indicted defendant for endangering the welfare of a child had sufficient evidence that defendant was "legally charged" with the care of Shanaya. We conclude that it did, because the evidence supported an inference that defendant was acting as the functional equivalent of Shanaya's parent at the relevant time.

According to evidence presented to the Grand Jury, Shanaya Jones on August 6, 1996, began an extended visit with her father and defendant, his wife. Defendant described herself, during Shanaya's visits, as the child's "mother," "stepmother" and "primary caretaker." Between August 14 and 16, Shanaya's father repeatedly punched the child, threw her into a wall and pushed her onto the floor, apparently because she would not eat. While defendant witnessed her husband inflict most of these beatings and was aware that the child had stopped eating, she did not seek medical attention until late in the evening of August 16, when Shanaya was brought by ambulance to a hospital emergency room. By the time the child arrived at the hospital, she had stopped breathing and had no pulse. After attempts to revive her were unsuccessful, she was pronounced dead.

An autopsy revealed that the cause of death was physical abuse sustained while at defendant's apartment. Shanaya's body was covered with bruises, lacerations, abrasions and hemorrhages. Several of her ribs were fractured and a lung was punctured. The Medical Examiner concluded that the injuries were days old, and that many of them would have been very painful, causing the child to scream and cry. The Examiner also determined that Shanaya was starved and dehydrated.

Defendant was charged with endangering the welfare of a child [N. Y. Penal Law, section 260.10 (2)]. Prior to trial, she moved to dismiss the indictment. Supreme Court granted the motion on the ground that there was insufficient evidence that defendant was "legally charged"--the statutory standard--with the care or custody of Shanaya. The Appellate Division reversed for two reasons.... We now affirm, solely on the first ground.

Pursuant to Penal Law 260.10 (2), "a parent, guardian or other person legally charged with the care or custody of a child less than eighteen years old" is guilty of endangering the welfare of a child if he or she "fails or refuses to exercise reasonable

4

diligence in the control of such child to prevent [the child] from becoming an 'abused child,' a 'neglected child,' a 'juvenile delinquent' or a 'person in need of supervision.'" One of the purposes of this statute is to establish "the duty of one parent to protect the child from the other parent."

Defendant argues that the proof before the Grand Jury was insufficient to show that she was legally charged with the care or custody of Shanaya, emphasizing that she was not Shanaya's biological mother, legal guardian or contractually hired care-giver. As for defendant's own statements to police that she acted as Shanaya's primary caretaker and mother during Shanaya's visits, defendant argues that they were inadequate to create a duty because they did not indicate that she had assumed all of the obligations of motherhood on a permanent basis. Penal Law 260.10 (2) specifically includes parents and guardians as people who are subject to prosecution. In effect, therefore, defendant argues that "other person legally charged with the care or custody of a child" is limited to people who have contracted to care for or who stand *in loco parentis* to a child. We conclude that the statutory term is not so narrowly confined.

Because the Penal Law does not describe who constitutes a "person legally charged with the care or custody of a child," defining this term falls to the courts. In discharging this responsibility, we are mindful of the statutory language, the legislative purpose and the Penal Law's directive that its provisions should be "construed according to the fair import of their terms to promote justice and effect the objects of the law" (Penal Law 5.00). In determining whether the evidence before the Grand Jury was legally sufficient to indict defendant, the court "must consider whether the evidence…would warrant conviction." Using this standard, the evidence before the Grand Jury established a *prima facie* case that defendant was legally responsible for Shanaya's and therefore legally charged with Shanaya's care under Penal Law 260.10 (2). Defendant's arguments regarding the actual extent of her involvement with the child might be issues for trial, but are not grounds for dismissal of the indictment. The Legislature could not possibly have intended a hired caretaker to be liable for endangering the welfare of a child [a holding from a prior case], but not a stepmother who functions in that role during the child's extended visits. [Affirmed.]

MULTIPLE CHOICE QUESTIONS

1. What is New York's penal code called?
   A. The Penal Code.
   B. The Criminal Procedure Law.
   C. The Penal Law.
   D. None of the above.

2. What is New York's highest court?
   A. The Appellate Court.
   B. The Court of Appeals.
   C. The Supreme Court.
   D. None of the above.

3. How many intermediate appellate courts are there in New York?
   A. One.
   B. Two.
   C. Three.
   D. Four.

4. The purpose of codifying criminal law is to:
   A. Ease the burden on judges and juries.
   B. Provide notice and due process to persons subject to criminal law.
   C. Provide victims with legal remedies.
   D. None of the above.

5. Early criminal law in the United States could be found in the:
   A. Penal codes.
   B. Common law.
   C. Criminal law codes.
   D. None of the above.

6. The common law is based on:
   A. Community standards.
   B. Legislative decisions.
   C. Jury decisions.
   D. None of the above.

7. The purpose of criminal law in New York is to:
   A. Deter crime.
   B. Rehabilitate offenders.
   C. Compensate victims.
   D. All the above.

8. Felony cases in New York are handled in the:
    A. County Court or Supreme Court.
    B. Court of Appeals.
    C. Circuit Court of trials.
    D. None of the above.

9. The intermediate appellate courts in New York are differentiated by calling them:
    A. District courts.
    B. Departments.
    C. Circuit Courts of Appeals.
    D. None of the above.

10. The proper name for a criminal law that prohibits robbery is a:
    A. Digest.
    B. Statute.
    C. Case reporter.
    D. None of the above.

11. A duty of care to a child can arise when:
    A. A person assumes a duty of care.
    B. A legal rule mandates a duty of care.
    C. A person enters into a contract to provide a duty of care.
    D. All the above.

12. A criminal statute should be read:
    A. Broadly.
    B. Narrowly.
    C. Expansively.
    D. All the above.

13. In New York, what is the institutional body that charges a defendant with a felony and thus holds the defendant for trial?
    A. A petit jury.
    B. A grand jury.
    C. A district court judge.
    D. All the above.

14. Every county in New York has:
    A. A Court of Appeals.
    B. A trial court.
    C. An Appellate Court.
    D. None of the above.

15. How many states have codified their criminal law to some extent?
    A. A minority of states.
    B. All the states.
    C. Twenty-five.
    D. None of the above.

16. What is the crime called when a person with a duty of care does not take appropriate steps to prevent harm from coming to a child?
    A. Conspiracy to harm a child.
    B. Endangering the welfare of a child.
    C. Child enticement.
    D. None of the above.

17. What is the section of the penal law that covers the correct answer to question number 16 above?
    A. 1.00.
    B. 1.05.
    C. 260.10(2).
    D. 420.13(4).

18. In People v. Carroll, the court held that:
    A. The conviction should be affirmed.
    B. The conviction should be reversed.
    C. The indictment stated a crime.
    D. The case should be dismissed.

19. In People v. Carroll, the defendant was:
    A. The victim's biological father.
    B. The victim's biological mother.
    C. The victim's childcare professional.
    D. None of the above.

20. In People v. Carroll, the case against the biological father would be tried in what court?
    A. The County Court or the Supreme Court.
    B. The Court of Appeals.
    C. The District Court.
    D. None of the above.

21. In People v. Burgh, the appellate court held that the trial court had failed to consider which of the purposes of New York's Penal Law:
    A. Deterrence
    B. Rehabilitation
    C. Public Safety
    D. All of the above

DISCUSSION EXERCISES

1. Which one of the purposes of New York's penal law discussed in the Burgh case should carry the most weight with a court that is deciding how to sentence a defendant?

2. How could one argue that the Court of Appeals was making "common law," and not adhering to the intent of the legislature in the Carroll case?

3. In enacting Penal Law 260.10(2), what was the purpose of the legislature as described in the Carroll case?

4. In deciding whether Penal Law 260.10(2) should be applied to the defendant, is it relevant that the defendant's prohibited conduct was a failure to act rather than an affirmative act?

5. How could the defendant in the Carroll case argue that she did not have fair notice that her omission would be a basis for criminal liability?

6. If the defendant in the Carroll case failed to do what the prosecution alleged she should have done, what would be the appropriate punishment?

Chapter Two

Constitutional Limits on Criminal Law

Introduction

Like all state penal codes, New York's Penal Law must not violate the United States Constitution or the New York State Constitution. The United States Constitution consists of seven Articles, which were ratified in 1789, and twenty-seven Amendments, which were ratified in the years since 1789. The Amendments include the first ten Amendments, commonly referred to as the "Bill or Rights," which were ratified in 1791. The Constitution protects citizens from certain governmental actions by ensuring that certain rights are preserved. With the exception of requiring the states and federal government to provide an attorney for every defendant who cannot afford one, however, the Constitution does not require the government to "give" any citizen anything of value (such as public assistance, education, or health care).

Article I of the Constitution protects individuals by prohibiting *ex post facto* laws and bills of attainder, while guaranteeing the writ of *habeas corpus*. An *ex post facto* law is a law that is passed after the commission of an act. An *ex post facto* law makes criminal today an act that was legal when it was committed yesterday. The prohibition on *ex post facto* laws is designed to ensure that the prior conduct, although perhaps unpopular, cannot be arbitrarily punished if the person who engaged in the conduct previously conformed her or his actions to the law. A bill of attainder is a legislatively enacted law that is designed to limit its application only to one or a few persons and inflict punishment on them without due process, such as a trial. In passing a bill of attainder, a legislature may simply decree that a person's conduct is criminal and then impose a punishment. *Habeas corpus* protects anyone in custody by allowing that person to contest the lawfulness of her or his custody or conditions of confinement in a federal court. [Articles II-VII of the United States Constitution deal with the structure of government.]

The first ten Amendments to the United States Constitution were ratified in 1791 and are often called "The Bill of Rights" because they provide many protections for individuals and criminal defendants. For example, the First Amendment allows individuals to express their opinions about government without fear of prosecution. The Fourth Amendment provides several procedural protections. The police cannot search persons, outside or inside their bodies (such as through blood and urine tests), or persons' homes, unless the police have a warrant issued by a judge based on probable cause to believe that the place or person to be searched can provide evidence of a crime. The Fifth Amendment protects what is commonly referred to as one's right to remain silent, but it also prevents a second trial of persons who have been found "not guilty" (the Double Jeopardy Clause) and ensures Due Process, as well as a Grand Jury Presentment for individuals facing federal prosecution. The Sixth Amendment ensures that every accused person may have a speedy trial and an attorney, including defendants who cannot afford an attorney. The Eighth Amendment prohibits excessive bail and cruel and unusual punishment. In addition, the Fourteenth Amendment, ratified in 1868, ensures that almost all the Bill of Rights protections in the first ten Amendments, which originally protected citizens against only the federal government, now protect citizens against each of the states.

Every state, including New York, has a state constitution. Many state constitutions contain provisions that are nearly identical to many provisions found in the federal constitution. For example, New York's Constitution contains a ban on cruel and unusual punishment that is very similar to the Eight Amendment to the United States Constitution. One practical reason for the inclusion of the identical provisions in state constitutions was that until the ratification of the Fourteenth Amendment in 1868 the Bill of Rights protections found in the first ten Amendments were not binding on the states. In their efforts to disperse powers among different governmental entities, the drafters of the federal Constitution were reluctant to usurp the powers of the states. As a result, in a federal prosecution, a defendant was entitled to all the Bill of Rights protections contained in the federal Constitution. The same defendant in a state prosecution, however, was entitled to none of the Bill of Rights protections, unless the defendant obtained protection through a state statute or state constitution.

In the 100 years following the ratification of the Fourteenth Amendment in 1868 (which followed the Civil War), and especially in the 1960s, the Supreme Court construed the Fourteenth Amendment as requiring the states to provide virtually all Bill of Rights protections to state defendants. Still, state defendants today do not have a federal constitutional right to have their cases presented to grand juries, to have a 12-person jury trial (except in death penalty cases), or to have a jury reach a unanimous verdict before finding the defendant guilty, although individual states can provide such rights under state constitutions or statutes.

The states need not provide defendants and citizens with more protections than the federal Constitution provides, although they can do so if they wish. In the 1960s, the Supreme Court found many protections for criminal defendants in the federal Constitution, but in the past several decades the Court has reversed this trend, refusing to find significant additional protections for criminal defendants in the federal Constitution. As a result, defendants today often cite state constitutions in arguing that they have additional rights and protections beyond those contained in the federal Constitution.

Void for Vagueness

Criminal statutes should be written clearly so that citizens know what conduct is prohibited. The concept of "void for vagueness" stems from statutes that are broadly worded. Those statutes use such vague and open-ended language that a reasonable person would not know precisely what conduct was prohibited. For example, a statute that makes "loitering" a criminal offense places in the individual police officer the authority to determine who can stand or walk in a particular place at a particular time (Papachristou v. Jacksonville, 405 U. S. 156 (1972)). Although no two circumstances are identical, even the most conscientious police officer may apply different standards to different people.

11

Placing such discretion in the hands of police officers can lead to arbitrary law enforcement.

Because New York City presents special challenges to law enforcement, some of which do not exist elsewhere in the country (such as challenges that occur within the subway system), the state of New York has implemented particular laws to deal with these challenges. In the case of People v. Nelson, below, the Court of Appeals determines how the void for vagueness doctrine applies in New York.

[You will note that in the Nelson case the Court of Appeals refers to "informations." An "information" is a legal document that lists the misdemeanor charges against a defendant. An indictment is the legal document that lists the felony charges against a defendant, although an indictment may also contain misdemeanor charges.]

People v. Nelson, 69 N.Y.2d 302, 506 N.E.2d 907, 514 N.Y.S.2d 197 (1987)

In People v Nelson et al., each of the defendants was charged with jostling (Penal Law 165.25) in Criminal Court informations. Police officers allegedly observed each of them patting down victims' pockets, reaching to purposely touch handbags, putting their hands into other people's pockets or crowding victims or acting as lookouts while their companions took these actions. On defendants' motions, Criminal Court dismissed the informations, holding the jostling statute void for vagueness. The Appellate Term reversed, denied defendants' motions to dismiss and reinstated the informations. ["A person is guilty of jostling when, in a public place, he intentionally and unnecessarily: 1. Places his hand in the proximity of a person's pocket or handbag; or 2. Jostles or crowds another person at a time when a third person's hand is in the proximity of such person's pocket or handbag."]

Defendant Tyler was convicted of jostling after a jury trial. The evidence presented to the jury indicated that defendant had placed his hands inside two of the pockets of a man who was lying drunk and asleep on a subway platform. The Appellate Term affirmed the conviction.

An officer allegedly observed defendant Robinson patting down two pockets of a sleeping subway passenger, placing his hands inside the man's pants pocket and attempting to remove money. Criminal Court dismissed the misdemeanor complaint on the ground that the People were required to submit a corroborating affidavit by the victim. The Appellate Term reversed, reinstated the accusatory instrument and remanded the matter for further proceedings.

On appeal, defendants argue primarily that the jostling statute is void for vagueness. A vagueness challenge involves a two-part analysis. First, it must be determined whether the statute in question is "sufficiently definite 'to give a person of ordinary intelligence fair notice that his contemplated conduct is forbidden by the statute'."

Citizens must be afforded fair warning of what is prohibited by law so that they may act accordingly. Second, a statute "'must provide explicit standards for those who apply them' so as to avoid 'resolution on an ad hoc and subjective basis, with the attendant dangers of arbitrary and discriminatory application'." The Constitution abhors a law placing unfettered discretion in the hands of police, prosecutors and juries and allowing punishment of the poor or unpopular on a whim (Papachristou v City of Jacksonville, 405 U.S. 156). Defendants allege that Penal Law 65.25 [prohibiting jostling] runs afoul of both of these concerns. We disagree.

Unlike statutes which have been declared void for vagueness because they provide insufficient warning to the person of ordinary intelligence, Penal Law 65.25 clearly delineates specific conduct easily avoided by the innocent-minded. It should present no difficulty for a citizen to comprehend that he must refrain from acting with the intent to bring his hand into the proximity of a stranger's pocket or handbag unnecessarily. Moreover, contrary to defendants' claim, the statute is no more difficult to interpret and obey because it does not require larcenous intent. Penal Law 165.25 prohibits a certain intentional course of conduct regardless of the wrongdoer's underlying purpose or motive.

Defendants concern themselves with possible applications of the word "unnecessarily" which would be outside the statute's intended realm, such as tugging on another's handbag to gain that person's attention. It has often been said, however, that, except in rare circumstances not relevant here, a vagueness challenge must be addressed to the facts before the court. Thus, if the actions of the defendants are plainly within the ambit of the statute, the court will not strain to imagine marginal situations in which the application of the statute is not so.

Here, defendants do not, nor could they, argue that their own acts should be interpreted as necessary. Therefore, any element of vagueness in this statute has had no effect on these defendants and they have no standing to complain of it. This court cannot consider the possibility that the statute may be vague as applied in other hypothetical situations.

Nor does Penal Law 165.25 encourage arbitrary or discriminatory application. The law, easily followed by most citizens of this State, provides objective criteria which must be observed by a police officer prior to arrest. It is not dependent upon the subjective conclusions of a complainant or an arresting officer as to what is annoying. This is not a statute which casts such a large net that it allows officials to round up those they have concluded to be undesirable. On the contrary, a person may be arrested pursuant to Penal Law 165.25 if the police have probable cause to believe, based upon observable conduct, that defendant unnecessarily and intentionally placed his hand in the proximity of another's pocket or handbag. [The orders of the Appellate Term should be affirmed.]

Equal Protection

New York's constitution contains an equal protection clause that is more expansive than that contained in the federal Constitution. In the federal Constitution, section 1 of the Fourteenth Amendment provides that no person shall be denied "equal protection of the laws." Essentially, this means that state governments (as well as the federal government by virtue of the 5th Amendment's Due Process Clause) must treat persons in similar circumstances the same.

New York's equal protection clause reads: No person shall be denied the equal protection of the laws of this state or any subdivision thereof. No person shall, because of race, color, creed or religion, be subjected to any discrimination in his civil rights by any other person or by any firm, corporation, or institution, or by the state or any agency or subdivision of the state. The Court of Appeals interprets New York's Equal Protection Clause in People v. Barnes, which is noted below. In essence, does a criminal conviction place someone in a "suspect class" such that the State must have compelling reasons before it can punish him (such as through a monetary fine), while not punishing or fining persons who have not been convicted of a crime?

People v. Barnes, 62 N.Y.2d 702, 465 N.E.2d 35, 476 N.Y.S.2d 528 (1984)

The defendant, having pleaded guilty to the class B misdemeanor of attempted resisting arrest, was sentenced to 90 days' imprisonment and a penalty assessment of $40. Defendant contends that the penalty assessment imposed under section 60.35 of the Penal Law…is civil in nature and is unconstitutional in that it discriminates against individuals who are convicted of Penal Law offenses in violation of the equal protection clauses of the State and Federal Constitutions.

Assuming, without deciding, that the mandatory penalty assessment law is civil in nature we conclude that it does not, as the defendant contends, offend the equal protection clause by creating an irrational classification. The statute treats all persons convicted of Penal Law offenses similarly, and it is of no moment that this group is singled out for this assessment. The "rational relationship" test sought to be applied by the defendant would only be relevant if the State sought to treat similarly situated individuals in a different manner. That is not the case here.

Because these statutes do not employ suspect classifications or adversely affect fundamental rights, the only rationality test which must be passed is the determination of "whether the challenged classification bears a reasonable relationship to some legitimate legislative objective." The penalty would appear to be related, at the very least, to the State's legitimate interest in raising revenues. [Order of the Appellate Term affirming the judgment of conviction is affirmed.]

Ex Post Facto Laws

An *ex post facto* law is a law, a statute for example, that is passed after the occurrence of the factual events that are the subject of a current criminal proceeding. The *ex post facto* statute changes how the law treats those factual events from the past. For example, assume that it was legal to possess balloons yesterday. If the legislature passes a criminal statute today that makes criminal the possession of balloons yesterday, then that statute serves to punish the balloon holder retroactively, who, yesterday, legally possessed the balloons. That statute is an example of an "*ex post facto* law," which is prohibited by the United States and New York Constitutions.

Retroactive punishment of legal actions serves few, if any, social purposes. [However, note the Nuremberg Trials following World War II for an illustration of why some commentators believe that *ex post facto* laws were used to convict and punish Nazis.] If people were punished today for their legal actions of yesterday, people would not engage in a variety of salutary and important activities in business, the arts, and many other areas of commerce. They would fear that their controversial activity, for example, might anger the legislature, which might seek to punish them at some time in the future through the passage of an *ex post facto* statute.

Moreover, an *ex post facto* law has little social value. It is true that an *ex post facto* law may actually serve sometimes as a potent general deterrent, because anything done today could be made illegal tomorrow. However, such laws would halt societal activity because most people would forego much of today's activity, which might be of great societal importance, for fear that the legislature tomorrow will not value such activity and will perhaps pass a criminal law that could result in conviction and imprisonment for that activity.

Examine the Weinberg case below, and analyze how the prohibition on *ex post facto* laws is applied in New York. In the Weinberg case, notice the importance of April 16, 1986 (never specifically mentioned in the case), the date on which the defendant's conduct (an omission—the failure to file tax returns) constituted the class E felony of "repeated failure to file a tax return." In essence, the defendant's failure to file a tax return by April 15, 1986 made his prior conduct (the failure to file tax returns in previous years) susceptible to greater punishment—as a felony for failure to file for several years.

People v. Weinberg, 83 N.Y.2d 262, 631 N.E.2d 97, 609N.Y.S.2d 155 (1994)

In January 1987, defendant was indicted for three misdemeanor counts of failure to file a tax return (Tax Law 1801) and one class E felony count of repeated failure to file a tax return (Tax Law 1802), arising from his failure to file New York State personal income tax returns for the years 1983, 1984 and 1985. In August 1987, eight months after he was indicted, defendant did file the delinquent returns. Defendant was ultimately convicted on all counts. Defendant appealed his conviction and the Appellate

Division affirmed (190 AD2d 767). A Judge of this Court granted defendant leave to appeal, and we now affirm.

Defendant's first point on appeal is that the Legislature did not intend Tax Law 1802 to be applied retroactively to a repeated failure to file returns which occurred in part prior to the effective date of the statute. The fatal flaw in this argument is that the statute is not being retroactively applied here in any true sense of the term. "A statute is not retroactive * * * when made to apply to future transactions, merely because such transactions relate to and are founded upon antecedent events."

Here, defendant "committed" the section 1802 offense when he failed to file his 1985 tax return by April 15, 1986, having then failed to file his returns for three consecutive years. Defendant's conduct thus falls within the plain statutory language concerning the applicability of the section, and he has pointed to no legislative history for the act in general or section 1802 in particular that would indicate otherwise. Defendant's construction—which would necessitate a conclusion that the Legislature did not intend for section 1802 to take effect for at least three years after its enactment—is further undermined by the Legislature's enactment of a companion bill providing for an immediate three-month, one-time-only tax amnesty period, whereby taxpayers were given the opportunity to settle their outstanding tax liabilities by paying back taxes and interest due the State. The immediate amnesty would have been meaningless as to section 1802 violations under defendant's construction that all nonfilings must occur after November 1, 1985.

Defendant's claim that Tax Law 1802 as applied against him in this case constitutes an unconstitutional *ex post facto* law is also without merit. As explained above, defendant did not commit the repeated failure to file offense until he failed to file his 1985 return by April 15, 1986, a point in time well after section 1802's effective date. As such, the Legislature has not punished defendant for acts previously committed that were innocent when performed, nor enhanced the punishment for a crime after its commission. Moreover, there is plainly absent here what the Supreme Court has identified as a "critical" element to relief under the *Ex Post Facto* Clause, "the lack of fair notice and governmental restraint when the legislature increases punishment beyond what was prescribed when the crime was consummated." Defendant, having failed to file returns for the two consecutive years of 1983 and 1984, was given fair warning by the enactment of section 1802 that his failure to file a return for 1985 would result in criminal liability for repeated failure to file under that section. We therefore conclude that defendant's prosecution under Tax Law 1802 does not violate the *ex post facto* prohibition. [Order of the Appellate Division affirmed.]

Free Speech

As one of the main communication centers in the world, New York and its residents have a long history of involvement in free speech cases, including those that have reached the Supreme Court. The Pentagon Papers case, involving the New York Times' publication of classified governmental documents critical of the government's role in the Vietnam War, helped to show that a prior restraint on the publication of information and news is highly disfavored and will almost never be approved (New York Times Co. v. United States, 403 U. S. 713 (1971)). The case of Feiner v. New York (340 U. S. 315 (1951)) helped illustrate that political speech can be prohibited only when it tends to cause immediate violence, such as an "incitement to riot," an event that is extremely rare. The case of New York Times v. Sullivan (376 U. S. 274 (1964)) established the requirement that plaintiffs alleging defamation (libel or slander) must show that the speaker or writer acted with the mental state of actual malice, or "reckless disregard" of the truth.

Perhaps accordingly, Article I, section 8, of the New York Constitution provides broad protection for speech, as follows:

> Every citizen may freely speak, write and publish his sentiments on all subjects, being responsible for the abuse of that right; and no law shall be passed to restrain or abridge the liberty of speech or of the press. In all criminal prosecutions or indictments for libels, the truth may be given in evidence to the jury; and if it shall appear to the jury that the matter charged as libelous is true, and was published with good motives and for justifiable ends, the party shall be acquitted; and the jury shall have the right to determine the law and the fact.

However, as illustrated in People v. Shack, below, not all speech is protected.

People v. Shack, 86 N.Y.2d 529, 658 N.E.2d 706, 634 N.Y.S.2d 660 (1995)

Defendant appeals from an order of the Appellate Term affirming his conviction, upon a jury verdict, of violating Penal Law 240.30(2), aggravated harassment in the second degree. The statute provides: "A person is guilty of aggravated harassment in the second degree when, with intent to harass, annoy, threaten or alarm another person, he ... [m]akes a telephone call, whether or not a conversation ensues, with no purpose of legitimate communication."

Defendant contends that the statute violates the United States and New York State Constitutions because it prohibits constitutionally protected speech, and because it violates his constitutional right to due process. We hold that the statute is not unconstitutional and find no merit in defendant's remaining contentions. Accordingly, the order of the Appellate Term should be affirmed.

I

Defendant Julian Shack suffers from mental illness, a fact which he concedes and which was the centerpiece of his defense at his trial. Complainant Diane Buffalin, defendant's first cousin, is a psychologist who lives and practices in Michigan. In June of 1990, defendant placed a telephone call to Buffalin at her home seeking information regarding his illness and medications and posing questions that arose from his treatment with a psychiatrist in New York. Buffalin, who had had no contact with defendant during the 12 years preceding this phone call, tried to answer his questions. Defendant apparently obtained some benefit from speaking with her, and upon his request she agreed to a continued telephone relationship with him, so long as he remained in treatment with his psychiatrist and continued taking his medication. From June through October, they spoke on the telephone approximately twice each week, and, during a visit to New York that summer, Buffalin "connected" defendant with an anxiety clinic at a New York City hospital.

Toward the end of October of 1990, defendant informed Buffalin that he was "doing better" and that he had stopped taking medication. She told him that because he was not taking his medication, she no longer welcomed his calls. In response, defendant advised Buffalin that if he ever got angry with her, he could burn down the house of her elderly father (his uncle), who lived in New York City. Through November and into December, defendant continued to call Buffalin. She repeatedly advised him that she did not want to speak with him if he was not taking his medication.

At the end of November, Buffalin informed defendant that she would be undergoing major surgery and told him not to call her during her two-week period of recuperation. On the day of her surgery, defendant called Buffalin three times, and he continued to place calls to her home repeatedly and regularly thereafter. From December 12 through the end of that month, he placed 88 phone calls to her home, sometimes calling as many as seven times a day. Defendant left messages on Buffalin's answering machine, asserting that if she refused to take his calls, he would begin to place repeated calls to her adult daughter, her mother-in-law and her father. In December, Buffalin wrote defendant a letter in which she tried to make it clear to him that his calls were unwanted, and she advised defendant that she would file a criminal complaint against him if he did not stop calling her.

Defendant continued to telephone Buffalin and records for his residence in Queens Country indicate 185 calls to her residence between December 12, 1990 and May 20, 1991. Defendant left messages in which he stated that if she refused to speak with him, he would sell her telephone number to a "pervert" who would delight in calling and upsetting her, that he would place dozens of phone calls to other family members and that he would call the Michigan licensing board to have her psychologist's license revoked. Buffalin telephoned defendant once in January to implore him to stop calling, and on several occasions she called him and replayed the taped messages of his calls so that he would know that evidence against him was being gathered. Nevertheless, defendant continued to place calls to Buffalin's home until May of 1991, when Buffalin came to New York and filed a criminal complaint against him. Defendant was arrested, prosecuted and convicted on one count of aggravated harassment in the second degree and sentenced to three years of probation.

Defendant challenges the constitutionality of the statute on several grounds.

18

Defendant's first claim is that the statute is facially unconstitutional because it impermissibly infringes the freedom of expression guaranteed by the First and Fourteenth Amendments of the Federal Constitution and article I, [section] 8 of the New York Constitution. Even if not facially unconstitutional, defendant maintains that it is unconstitutional as applied to him.

Penal Law 240.30(2) does not prohibit speech or expression—on its face, its proscription is limited to conduct (making a telephone call without any legitimate purpose of communication). The limiting clause which expressly excludes constitutionally protected speech from its reach plainly distinguishes this statute from those which impose criminal liability for "pure speech;" Cohen v California, 403 US 15, 18 [an epithetic phrase worn on a jacket was not "offensive conduct"]. Accordingly, because Penal Law 240.30 (2) proscribes only conduct and expressly removes from its application "legitimate communication," defendant may not invoke the First Amendment or article I, [section] 8 of the State Constitution to support a challenge to the facial validity of the statute.

Moreover, even if Penal Law 240.30 (2) is construed to proscribe speech, a declaration of facial overbreadth does not automatically follow. Constitutional free speech protections "have never been thought to give absolute protection to every individual to speak whenever or wherever he pleases, or to use any form of address in any circumstances that he chooses"; a person's right to free expression may be curtailed "upon a showing that substantial privacy interests are being invaded in an essentially intolerable manner." An individual's right to communicate must be balanced against the recipient's right "to be let alone" in places in which the latter possesses a right of privacy, or places where it is impractical for an unwilling listener to avoid exposure to the objectionable communication.

Under some circumstances, the privacy right may "plainly outweigh" the free speech rights of an intruder. Manifestly, an individual has a substantial privacy interest in his or her telephone. The statute is narrowly drafted and furthers the State's compelling interest in protecting its citizens from "persons who employ the telephone, not to communicate, but for other unjustifiable motives."

Nor is the statute unconstitutional as applied to defendant, because it did not subject him to criminal liability for engaging in protected speech; his liability arose from his harassing conduct, not from any expression entitled to constitutional protection. Although defendant claims that he had a legitimate purpose because he placed his calls seeking help for his illness, that argument addresses only those telephone calls placed before Buffalin told him to stop calling her. The manner and substance of defendant's calls changed dramatically in December, and the information charged him with criminal conduct only after that time. In sum, we conclude that Penal Law 240.30 (2) does not violate the constitutional right to free speech. Accordingly, the order of the Appellate Term should be affirmed.

19

Cruel and Unusual Punishment

While citizens and criminal defendants in the United States probably enjoy more civil liberties than people in any other country, they can face exceptional punishment for criminal convictions. Unlike all other western countries, the United States permits the death penalty. Currently 38 states, including New York, have statutes that permit the death penalty for certain types of murder. Although Article I, section 5, of the New York Constitution prohibits "cruel and unusual punishments," New York statutory law permits the death penalty to be imposed for specific types of murder (Penal Law 125.27), such as the murder of a police officer and deaths resulting from the commission of certain crimes, including rape and burglary. However, the New York Court of Appeals has not ruled on the constitutionality of the death penalty under Article I, section 5 of the New York Constitution. Since 1976, the methods of execution have consisted of electrocution, lethal injection, hanging, and firing squad. If the Court of Appeals finds the death penalty permissible under the New York Constitution, the method of execution will be lethal injection.

See People v. Broadie, noted below, for an example of a statute that permits life imprisonment for a drug offense. Note that in New York a defendant must serve the minimum portion of her or his sentence, at which time the defendant is eligible for parole. However, if parole is denied repeatedly, the defendant could theoretically serve a term of life imprisonment. That is, he or she could stay in prison until death.

In the Broadie case, the defendants faced life sentences for selling drugs. Under the so-called "Rockefeller Drug Laws" (passed by the legislature under former Governor Rockefeller), New York authorizes some of the most severe sentences in the country for the sale of drugs. In reading the Broadie case, ask whether a life sentence for selling drugs is cruel and unusual punishment. If you think that a life sentence does not constitute cruel and unusual punishment, consider whether a life sentence is disproportionate to the crime in relation to the sentences other defendants receive for other crimes. For example, the maximum possible punishment for manslaughter, such as when a defendant kills someone while under extreme emotional disturbance, is "only" 25 years in prison, with parole eligibility after 8 1/3 years.

People v. Broadie, 37 N.Y.2d 100, 332 N.E.2d 338, 371 N.Y.S.2d 471 (1975)

[Many defendants were part of this consolidated appeal. They challenged statutes that classified the crime of drug selling as the most serious category of crime in New York and sentences that imposed a mandatory maximum sentence of life imprisonment and minimums from one or six year to eight and one-third years.] In each case, the Appellate Division sustained the statutes as constitutional.

The principal issue is whether the so-called "drug" laws, in mandating life imprisonment and, therefore, lifetime parole on parole release, prescribe sentences so disproportionate as would constitute cruel and unusual punishment in violation of constitutional limitations (New York Constitution, art. I, 5; US Constitution, 8th Amendment). Of course, defendants in these cases are not being punished for their status as addicts but for the offenses they have committed, however impelled by their "drug dependency," if that were the cause of their criminal acts. In a deterministic sense, all criminals commit the crimes they do because they "must."

There should be an affirmance. The sentences are not grossly disproportionate in constitutional analysis. The Legislature may distinguish among the ills of society which require a criminal sanction, and prescribe, as it reasonably views them, punishments appropriate to each. Thus, while the courts possess the power to strike down punishments as violative of constitutional limitations, the power must be exercised with especial restraint. However disproportionality is measured, the instant sentences do not rise to the gross disproportionality violative of constitutional limitations. The constitutional equal protection (NY Const, art I, 11; US Const, 14th Amendment) arguments of appellants are not separately discussed because the same reasoning which supports the concededly and intendedly severe sentences, especially with regard to deterrence, would sustain, if valid, a reasonable classification between defendants in drug cases and in other cases.

No punishment in this State has ever been struck down as unconstitutionally disproportionate to its crime. Courts of this State have nevertheless recognized the principle of gross disproportionality. Elsewhere, even in the United States Supreme Court, this principle has been considered applicable, and, in some instances, has been used to overturn statutory punishments. Given the flexibility of the cruel and unusual punishment clause, and the persuasive, if not circular, logic of the assertion that grossly disproportionate punishments are "cruel and unusual," the applicability of the principle is here accepted.

Apart from a subjective evaluation which looks to the extent to which the conscience of the court is shocked by punishments imposed, there have developed standards to determine whether punishments are constitutionally disproportionate. Because such a subjective test has obvious weaknesses in trying to apply a rational analysis, although often used by such of the courts which have applied or discussed the cruel and unusual punishments clause, there will be no discussion of it.

The gravity of the offense is obviously key, as is the gravity of the danger which the offender poses to society. Given grave offenses committed or committable by dangerous offenders, the penological purposes of the sentencing statutes, whether they be the rehabilitation or isolation of offenders or the deterrence of potential offenders, will be decisive.

In assessing the gravity of a criminal offense, the primary consideration is the harm it causes to society. The Legislature, in making this assessment, could properly view criminal narcotics sales not as a series of isolated transactions, but as symptoms of the widespread and pernicious phenomenon of drug distribution. Social harm in drug distribution is great indeed. The drug seller, at every level of distribution, is at the root of the pervasive cycle of destructive drug abuse.

Defendants would minimize drug trafficking by arguing that it is not a crime of violence. Because of their illegal occupation, however, drug traffickers do often commit crimes of violence against law enforcement officers and, because of the high stakes, engage in crimes of violence among themselves [two drug pushers, upon learning of a dealer's plot to have one kill the other, kill the dealer].

More significant, of course, are the crimes which drug traffickers engender in others. The seller often introduces the future addict to narcotics. The addict, to meet the seller's price, often turns to crime to "feed" his habit. Narcotics addicts not only account for a sizable percentage of crimes against property; they commit a significant number of crimes of violence as well.

Thus the Legislature could reasonably have found that drug trafficking is a generator of collateral crime, even violent crime. And violent crime is not, of course, the only destroyer of men and the social fabric. Drug addiction degrades and impoverishes those whom it enslaves. This debilitation of men, as well as the disruption of their families, the Legislature could also lay at the door of the drug traffickers. Measured thus by the harm it inflicts upon the addict, and, through him, upon society as a whole, drug dealing in its present epidemic proportions is a grave offense of high rank.

A second consideration, in assessing the proportionality of the punishment to the crime, is the character of the offender and the gravity of the threat he poses to society. None of the present cases involve what are often called "accidental" offenders. True, not all of these defendants are "hardened" criminals. In each case, however, defendant was convicted of at least "street" sales of heroin or cocaine, or possession of a large amount of narcotics, two of the situations to which the statutes were directed.

The penological purposes, conceived by the Legislature as justifying the elimination of discretionary, individualized sentencing in favor of inflexible maximum lifetime sentences, are additional factors to be considered in measuring disproportionality.

Defendants argue that the new sanctions neither favor, nor presume much likelihood of, their future rehabilitation. True, the elimination of discretionary sentencing, and the substitution of inflexible maximum sentences have been often tried and as often abandoned as "remedies." Equally true, there is considerable highly-respected authority which questions the wisdom of eliminating flexible sentencing standards in.

Rehabilitation, however, is only one of the recognized purposes of penal sanctions. At the same time, put aside as factors are motives of retribution or stimulus to vigilantism which sometimes may avowedly or unconsciously motivate the use of criminal sanctions. Faced with what it found to be a high recidivism rate in drug-related crimes, an inadequate response to less severe punishment, and an insidiously growing drug abuse problem, the

Legislature could reasonably shift the emphasis to other penological purposes, namely, isolation and deterrence.

The reasons for isolating drug traffickers have already been suggested. The Legislature could find that narcotics sellers were the crucial link in the pernicious cycle of drug abuse; that sellers spawn addiction, and that addicts, in turn, may become sellers. As a minimal proposition, the seller, in feeding the addict's habit, frustrates rehabilitation. The Legislature could conclude that the best way to break the chain would be to remove the seller from society for a long duration, and, upon his return, to continue surveillance through lifetime parole.

Deterrence is the other obvious purpose. It was thought that rehabilitation efforts had failed; that the epidemic of drug abuse could be quelled only by the threat of inflexible, and therefore certain, exceptionally severe punishment. Thus, to achieve the deterrence, so far seemingly elusive, the would-be drug trafficker had to be put on notice that, should he be caught, his fate was sealed regardless of his position in the hierarchy of distribution and regardless of the quantity of drugs in which he dealt.

The drug offenses, concededly, are punished more severely and inflexibly than almost any other offense in the State. Only for murder in the first degree is a greater penalty, capital punishment, prescribed by statute. Among class A felonies, the narcotics offenses alone may not be reduced below the class A-III level by plea negotiations. Among class A felony offenders, only those convicted of sale or possession of narcotics are barred from being absolutely discharged from their sentences after five years' unrevoked parole. In comparison with other jurisdictions, drug trafficking is punished more severely in this State than in other jurisdictions.

Summarizing the various factors and comparisons pertinent to gross disproportionality, the Legislature could reasonably conclude that drug trafficking was a grave offense; that the defendants, as sellers, posed a serious threat to society; and that the sentencing statutes, though severe and inflexible, would serve, at least, to isolate and deter. Compared both "internally," to punishments for other crimes under the Penal Law, and "externally," to punishments imposed elsewhere for the same or similar offenses, the narcotics laws are relatively severe, but not irrationally so, given the epidemic dimensions of the problem.

In this analysis, the punishments in these cases were not so grossly disproportionate that they may be declared unconstitutional. Rarely has a penal sanction been struck down by the courts of this State as unconstitutional under the cruel and unusual punishments clause, and never on the ground of disproportionality. Accordingly, the orders of the Appellate Divisions should be affirmed.

MULTIPLE CHOICE QUESTIONS

1. When was the Fourteenth Amendment ratified?
   A. 1789.
   B. 1791.
   C. 1868.
   D. 1964.

2. What right need the states not provide to criminal defendants?
   A. An attorney.
   B. A grand jury.
   C. A trial.
   D. None of the above.

3. If a state statute that is enacted in 2001 prohibits for the first time the smoking of marijuana in 1999, the statute is:
   A. Void for vagueness.
   B. An equal protection violation.
   C. An *ex post facto* law.
   D. Constitutionally permitted.

4. What United States Constitutional right does a defendant not have?
   A. Grand jury.
   B. Twelve person jury.
   C. Unanimous jury verdict.
   D. All the above.

5. A law that is void for vagueness in New York is:
   A. Loitering.
   B. Telephone harassment.
   C. Filing late tax returns.
   D. None of the above.

6. The crime of "jostling" is:
   A. Void for vagueness.
   B. An *ex post facto* law.
   C. A violation of free speech.
   D. None of the above.

7. The equal protection clause in the New York Constitution is _____ than the equal protection clause in the United States Constitution.
   A. Narrower.
   B. Broader.
   C. Shorter.
   D. None of the above.

8. In People v. Nelson, the court held that:
   A. The defendant's telephone calls were protected speech.
   B. The defendant's telephone calls were not protected speech.
   C. Jostling is not a crime.
   D. None of the above.

9. In People v. Weinberg, the court held that:
   A. Tax laws do not violate the equal protection clause.
   B. Tax laws do not violate the *ex post facto* clause.
   C. Tax laws do not violate the void for vagueness clause.
   D. Tax laws do not violate the free speech clause.

10. In People v. Shack, the court held that:
    A. The defendant's telephone calls were protected speech.
    B. The defendant's telephone calls were not protected speech.
    C. Jostling is not a crime.
    D. None of the above.

11. The death penalty may be imposed in New York for:
    A. Robbery.
    B. A Rape that results in the death of the victim.
    C. Manslaughter.
    D. None of the above.

DISCUSSION EXERCISES

1. If the Nuremberg trials, where Nazis were tried for various crimes enacted after World War II, had been held under New York law, what would have been the Nazi's best constitutional defense, and why?

2. Describe a fact situation in which the defendant could not be prosecuted for speaking even where another person wanted him to stop.

3. Write a law that would be "void for vagueness."

4. Describe the reasoning behind why the Bill of Rights did not originally apply to the states.

5. Why would the framers of the United States and New York Constitutions include a "double jeopardy" clause?

6. How specific must a law be before the State can claim that the law gives us clear notice of what conduct the law prohibits? In the Nelson case, the Court of Appeals refers to a "jostling" statute that prohibits "placing one's hands in another person's pocket or handbag" and includes "crowding a person [a victim] when a third person's hand is in the proximity of the victim's pocket or handbag." Does this statute cover "innocent" actions, such as circumstances that occur in a crowded subway car?

7. In People v. Shack, is the Court of Appeals' reasoning convincing, in that repeated telephone calls constitute "conduct" and not speech? The court says that "Penal Law 240.30(2) does not prohibit speech or expression--on its face, its proscription is limited to conduct (making a telephone call without any legitimate purpose of communication)." Does the court provide a definition or rule that allows us to determine the difference between "conduct" and expression? Under the court's reasoning, could Penal Law 240.30(2) prohibit repeatedly walking with a sign on the sidewalk in front of a residence or business and holding a sign that indicates the same words that the defendant Shack said in his numerous telephone calls to his cousin?

8. In this chapter, you learned that drug sentences can be even more severe than sentences for homicide. Do you believe drug dealing or manslaughter is a greater social harm?

Chapter Three

The General Principles of Criminal Liability

Introduction

In New York, every crime is defined by the legislature in the form of a statute. A statute is a rule passed by the legislature and approved by the governor. Almost all criminal statutes are contained in the Penal Law. Every statute contains various elements, which are the components of a crime. Four basic elements exist. They are the <u>act</u> (or *actus reus*) that the defendant committed (including omissions); the <u>mental state</u> (or *mens rea*) with which the defendant acted; the fact that the defendant <u>caused</u> (or causation) the act; and the <u>result</u> that the defendant caused. For example, a defendant who pulls the trigger of a loaded gun with the intent that his victim will die and thus causes a bullet to enter and cause the death of the victim is guilty of an intentional homicide ("murder") in violation of Penal Law 125.25(1). The act and the mental state elements will be discussed below.

The Act or *Actus reus*

The requirement that every statute (or crime) contain the element of an act can be a misnomer. In reality, the act or *actus reus* element contains three components. The most obvious component is an action, described by the Penal Law (15.00) as a "voluntary act," such as pulling the trigger of a gun. Also, an additional type of action may be characterized as "possession." For example, if someone carries a loaded gun illegally (Penal Law 265.02(4)) in her pocket and a police officer stops and searches her for some legitimate reason and finds the gun, the person with the gun has not committed some "action" at the moment (albeit she placed the gun in her pocket at some previous point in time). Nonetheless, the person's possession has satisfied the *actus reus* element (Penal Law 15.00(2)).

A third component of the *actus reus* element is an "omission." An omission is a failure to act when someone has a duty to act (Penal Law 15.00(3)). For example, if a parent, or a police officer, or a lifeguard assumes the responsibility (by giving birth or by agreeing to perform certain duties) to care for a child or the citizenry in general and then does nothing (an omission), with no risk of danger to one's self, to save a child who is in danger of death, for example, then the person with the duty probably would be guilty of some homicide if the child died.

Except perhaps in regard to strict liability crimes (discussed below), in all circumstances, the *actus reus* element must be voluntary before it can constitute an element of a criminal offense. A voluntary act means "a bodily movement performed consciously as a result of effort or determination." To illustrate, if drug dealers kidnapped a victim and placed cocaine in the victim's pocket, the victim could be said to "possess" an illegal substance. Nonetheless, the victim would not be guilty of possessing the cocaine "illegally," because the victim did not possess the cocaine voluntarily and thus did not commit one of the essential elements of the crime (a voluntary *actus reus*).

Use the People v. Newton case (a decision by a trial court judge, not an appellate court), noted below, to analyze what is a voluntary act. Determine what component of the *actus reus* element was at issue in the case.

People v. Newton, 72 Misc.2d 646, 340 N.Y.S.2d 77 (1973)

[Defendant] comes before this court to enforce his civil right to liberty. He resorts to the great writ of *habeas corpus* which has for centuries been the only real and sufficient bastion of personal freedom and dignity. He inquires not into the offense charged to him but into the esteemed right to liberty which is the matrix of our judicial system. The instant writ tests the legality of petitioner's detention, notwithstanding the criminal act he is alleged to have committed.

The sole issue to be decided by this court is one of jurisdiction over the person of the petitioner. On December 7, 1972 petitioner boarded Air International Bahamas' flight No. 101 bound from the Bahamas to Luxembourg. While on board, the petitioner had concealed on his person a loaded .38 caliber revolver and a quantity of ammunition. At some time during the flight, the captain became aware of the fact that petitioner might possibly be carrying a firearm. There is some indication that the petitioner, severely handicapped and ambulatory only with the aid of prosthetic devices, caused himself to be unruly. The extent to which petitioner was unruly on board the plane, if in fact he was, cannot be ascertained from the evidence before the court. Suffice it to say that the captain of flight No. 101, for reasons best known to himself, saw fit to interrupt the course of the plane which was flying over international waters and effected a landing in the County of Queens at the John F. Kennedy International Airport. The landing was made at approximately 12:35 a.m. on December 8, 1972. Officers from the Port Authority Police Department, in response to a radio transmission, went to the runway where the plane, with petitioner on board, was waiting. One of the officers boarded the plane, approached the defendant-petitioner, and inquired of him as to whether or not he had a weapon. The petitioner answered that he did have a weapon which he allowed to be removed from his person. He was then arrested and charged with a violation of subdivision 2 of section 265.05 of the Penal Law of the State of New York after his admission that he had no license to possess or carry the weapon in question. Subdivision 2 of section 265.05 of the Penal Law is as follows: "Any person who has in his possession any firearm which is loaded with ammunition, or who has in his possession any firearm and, at the same time, has in his possession a quantity of ammunition which may be used to discharge such firearm is guilty of a class D felony."

Intent is not an element of the crime of possessing, without a license, a loaded pistol or revolver which might be concealed on the person of an accused. Guilty knowledge, or scienter is not an element of the crime of unlawful possession of a firearm. "The minimal requirement for criminal liability is the performance by a person of conduct which includes a voluntary act or the omission to perform an act which he is physically capable of performing." (Penal Law 15.10). The doing of an act may by statute be made criminal without regard to the doer's intent or knowledge, but an involuntary action is not criminal.

The court finds that the petitioner, William Jesse Newton, Jr., did not subject himself to criminal liability by virtue of a voluntary act. Flight No. 101 was not scheduled to terminate in or pass through the territorial jurisdiction of the United States. The landing at John F. Kennedy International Airport on December 8, 1972 was merely an interruption of flight not attributable to a voluntary action by the petitioner. No documentary evidence or official records are before this court to indicate anything to the contrary. This court will not create jurisdiction where none exists, solely on the basis of a fortuitous happening. It is therefore, the opinion of this court that the writ of *habeas corpus* be sustained and the petitioner be discharged from custody forthwith.

Mental State or *Mens rea*

To be guilty of a crime, a defendant must always commit an action with a specific "culpable mental state" (Penal Law 15.05) (with the exception of strict liability and vicarious liability crimes, discussed below). That is, at the time of the defendant's action, he or she must exhibit one of the culpable mental states, which in New York are: intent, knowledge, recklessness, and criminal negligence (Penal Law 15.05(1-4)), and also depraved indifference in murder cases (Penal Law 125.25(2)).

For the public policy purpose of limiting criminal liability, the defendant's action and mental state must usually occur simultaneously. To illustrate, if Driver A drives so carelessly that he causes Driver B to drive into a ditch, then Driver B may develop "road rage" and become angry and intentionally try to kill Driver A. Assume that Driver B is unsuccessful in an attempt to kill Driver A and that Driver B no longer wants Driver A to die. Two days later, Driver B herself is driving carelessly and, without realizing she is driving anyone off the road, causes Driver A, who is in his car, to run into a wall and die.

If not for the requirement that the *actus reus* and the mental state (or *mens rea*) occur simultaneously, Driver B could be guilty of an intentional homicide for causing the death of Driver A today, even though she did not realize that she was driving carelessly or that Driver A was the person in the other car. [Driver B might be guilty of a negligent homicide.] A general purpose of the criminal law is to hold liable only persons who were aware of their conduct or should have been aware of their conduct; thus, it would seem unfair to hold Driver B liable for an intentional killing of Driver A when she did not even realize that her driving would cause harm to anyone.

The penalty that is attached to criminal offenses in New York is determined by the defendant's mental state. The culpable mental states in New York may be illustrated by using criminal homicide as an example (Penal Law 125.00). For instance, the most venal mental state (when accompanied, of course, by an action) is "intention." A person acts intentionally when her or his conscious objective is to cause a certain result (Penal Law

15.05(1), such as death in homicide cases. Thus, the husband who kills his wife for the proceeds of her insurance policy by running her down with a car at 35 miles per hour would be guilty of an intentional homicide (Murder in the Second Degree under Penal Law 125.25(1)).

In many instances, the mental state of "knowledge" can be considered as venal as intent. A person acts knowingly when he or she is aware of his conduct (Penal Law 15.05(2)) and the repercussions that can flow from it. For example, assume that a naturally "mean" automobile driver sees many people crossing the street but decides to close his eyes and drive toward the people at 35 miles per hour. The driver is aware that a death could ensue from his actions. If a death did occur, this driver could probably be said to have acted with knowledge, or "depraved indifference," which in New York is a rough equivalent of knowledge. The driver could be convicted of Murder in the Second Degree (Penal Law 125.25(2)). [New York does not have a homicide offense based on "knowledge."]

The third culpable mental state in New York is "recklessness." A person acts recklessly when he or she is "aware of and consciously disregards a substantial and unjustified risk that a certain result will occur." For example, assume that two people steal a car because they have no car of their own and want to drive fast around town. The person in the passenger seat tells the driver of the stolen to car to slow down because they are approaching a school near the end of the school day and they do not want to injure any children. The driver says, "I realize this, but I like driving fast, and I don't plan on killing any kids." The driver, who will become a defendant, drives on regardless. In a 5 mile per hour zone, the defendant is driving 35 miles per hour. A child enters the cross walk, but, because of the speed of the car, the driver cannot stop before hitting and killing the child. The driver would have recklessly caused the death and be guilty of Manslaughter in the Second Degree (125.15(1)).

The least culpable mental state is termed "criminal negligence." A person acts with criminal negligence when he or she "fails to perceive a substantial and unjustified risk" that certain actions will cause a certain result (Penal Law 15.05(4)). For example, a person may not see or hear well enough to drive a car without causing an accident. However, this person may be unaware of her sight and hearing deficits because she has refused to see her doctor. If this person drives her car at 35 miles per hour but is unable to see the pedestrian in the sidewalk and then runs over and kills the pedestrian, the driver would have acted with criminal negligence and be guilty of Criminally Negligent Homicide under Penal Law 125.10.

The determination of the mental state with which a defendant acted is critical, because sentences in criminal cases, such as prison terms, are meted out on the basis of the defendant's culpability, which is determined by noting the defendant's mental state. For instance, in the homicide cases above, every driver was driving 35 miles per hour, and every driver caused the death of another person. The only distinguishing element among the homicides was the mental state of the defendants. Based on the culpable mental states of the defendants, the Penal Law (70.00) provides for vastly different punishments. The husband who intentionally killed his wife and the mean driver who drove into the crowd would receive a minimum of 15 years in prison (before eligibility for parole) and a maximum of life, or perhaps even death. The car thief who killed the child could be sentenced to no imprisonment or to a maximum of 15 years in prison. The sight and hearing impaired person who did not see the pedestrian that she killed could be sentenced to no imprisonment or to a maximum of four years in prison.

Sometimes the distinction between mental states, such as "recklessness," and "criminal negligence" can be difficult to determine. In the following case, consider whether the court clearly explained the difference between these two mental states. The defendant was charged with manslaughter in the second degree.

People v. Strong, 45 A.D.2d 18, 356 N.Y.S.2d 200 (4th Department 1974)

Defendant, 57 years old, claims to be the leader in the United States of a religious sect known as Sudan Muslims, the central belief and practice of which is that the mind has power over matter, including the body. He had about 70 followers in Rochester, Kenneth Goins being one of them. He asserted that he had the power temporarily to cause one's heart to stop and the blood to cease flowing in such person's veins, and to do other supernatural acts. He claimed that he had done such feats for 40 years without injury to a "follower." To demonstrate the efficacy of his religion and his power, it was defendant's practice to hold meetings and to put a follower through what he called "a submission." There was evidence that during such a submission he had stuck as many as five knives into a follower without injury.

On January 28, 1972 defendant conducted such a demonstration in Rochester, and it appears that Goins volunteered to go through the ritual. Defendant testified that he first administered a prayer rite to Goins and "suspended" him so that he had no heart beat or pulse and he ceased breathing; that he then placed three knives and a hatchet in his body; that one of the knives was placed in the center of Goins' chest to a depth of two and a-half inches. When he removed the knives and hatchet Goins began to bleed from his chest, and despite all efforts to stanch the flow, Goins died. One of defendant's followers who was present at this demonstration testified that on previous demonstrations by defendant she had seen the victims bleeding a little. She testified that on the night in question, before defendant inserted the knives in Goins, Goins said to defendant, "No, Father," and defendant replied, "It will be all right, son."

A medical examiner who performed an autopsy on Goins' body testified that one of the stab wounds penetrated Goins' heart and was four and three-quarters inches deep, and that it was the cause of his death.

On these facts did the trial court err in declining to charge that the jury could find defendant guilty of a lesser crime than manslaughter second degree, to wit, criminally negligent homicide?

A person is guilty of manslaughter in the second degree when he "recklessly" causes the death of another person (Penal Law 125.15, subd. 1). A person acts "recklessly" with respect to a result when he is aware of and consciously disregards a substantial and unjustifiable risk that such result will occur (Penal Law 15.05, subd. 3).

A person is guilty of criminally negligent homicide when, with "criminal negligence," he causes the death of another person (Penal Law 125.10). A person acts with "criminal negligence" with respect to a result when he fails to perceive a substantial and unjustifiable risk that such result will occur (Penal Law 15.05, subd. 4).

The distinction between manslaughter in the second degree and criminally negligent homicide lies in whether there is a conscious disregard of the result or only a failure to perceive the risk of the result.... The distinction between reckless conduct and criminally negligent conduct involves the mental state required for each, and not the nature of the risk. The reckless offender is aware of the proscribed risk and consciously disregards it. The criminally negligent offender, on the other hand, is not aware of the risk created and, therefore, cannot be guilty of consciously disregarding it....

Defendant contends that his frame of mind at the time of the act was such that he did not believe that Goins would be killed by placing the knife into him. Thus, it is defendant's contention that he was not aware of the risk involved and that he failed to perceive any risk. This being so, defendant argues that the court erred in refusing to charge the lesser crime of criminally negligent homicide....

On no view of the evidence in this record is there warrant for a verdict of guilty of criminally negligent homicide, since there is no basis on which the jury could have found that defendant failed to perceive the risk inherent in his actions. Defendant unequivocally admitted to stabbing Goins in the chest at least to a depth of two and a half inches. To suggest that Goins' death was the result of negligence simply defies logic and common sense. Defendant's belief in his superhuman powers whether real or simulated, did not result in his failure to perceive the risk, but, rather, led him consciously to disregard the risk of which he was aware. A verdict finding such a conscious disregard of a substantial and unjustifiable risk was the only verdict that the jury could return on the evidence in this record....

Accordingly, the trial court properly refused to charge that the jury could find defendant guilty of the lesser crime of criminally negligent homicide, and the judgment should be affirmed.

Strict Liability

In a few instances, a defendant can be deemed liable for a crime even though the defendant exhibited no culpable mental state. Assuming that the legislature's intent (Penal Law 15.15(2)) was not to include a culpable mental state (intent, knowledge, recklessness, or criminal negligence) as one of the elements of a statute, such a statute should be characterized as creating a "strict liability" crime (Penal Law 15.10). The purpose of a strict liability crime is to discourage a particularly harmful behavior by providing severe punishment solely for an action, even one unaccompanied by any culpable mental state.

The classic example of a strict liability crime is "statutory rape," a crime that legislatures have created to deter adults from having sexual relations with children. Thus, in New York, any person older than 21 years who has sexual intercourse with anyone younger than 17 years (even though the person under 17 has consented to sexual intercourse) could be guilty of Rape in the Third degree (Penal Law 130.25(2)), a Class E felony that is punishable by up to four years in prison. In the Dozier case, below, the court describes the legislature's reasons for making statutory rape a strict liability crime. [Note that this case involves an earlier version of the statute, which distinguished between males and females under the age of 17 years].

People v. Dozier, 72 A.D.2d 478, 424 N.Y.S.2d 1010 (1st Department 1980)

Convicted, upon his plea of guilty, of rape in the third degree, in that being over the age of 21 years, he had sexual intercourse with a female less than 17 years of age (Penal Law 130.25, subd 2), defendant challenges New York's statutory rape law as violative of due process and equal protection. Specifically, defendant claims that the statute offends constitutional precepts because it does not permit ignorance, fraud or mistake as to the female's age to be asserted as a defense....

In support of his due process challenge defendant claims that complainant, before engaging in sexual relations with him, showed him an identification card which represented that she was 18 years of age, and that had he known that she was not even 17 he would have refrained from having intercourse with her.

We find that the statute serves a significant State interest in that it protects a certain class of minors from any adverse consequences of sexual intercourse, even if consensual. Following long-settled principles, we also find no constitutional prohibition against imposing criminal liability for conduct in which *Mens rea* is not an element of the offense.

The question for resolution then is whether the prevention of sexual intercourse by unmarried females under 17 serves a significant State interest not present when the proscribed activity is undertaken by females 17 years of age and older.... The focus of inquiry, therefore, must be directed to the nature of the State's interest, if any, in prohibiting sexual intercourse by unwed females under 17, and the reasonableness of age 17 as the line of demarcation between consensual incapacity and a female's right to sexual freedom equal to that of her male consort.

Two immediate interests come to mind. First, and most obvious, is the problem of preventing pregnancy. "Along with pregnancy comes all of the attendant psychological, medical, sociological, and moral problems, including questions of whether to have an abortion or to bear the child." Secondly, although many females under 17, such as those in prepubescence, are physically incapable of childbearing, younger girls, at the same time, are susceptible to physical injury resulting from sexual intercourse....

The State has a legitimate concern that females 16 years and younger do not become pregnant or suffer physical injury, and as a result, find themselves facing practical problems for which their youth has not prepared them. Forced marriage, unwed motherhood, adoption, abortion, the need for medical treatment and precipitate withdrawal from school are just some of the considerations which often have to be faced, so it can be discerned that the State's concern stems from more than a dogmatic insistence on appropriate adolescent behavior.

Adolescence is a period of physical and emotional turbulence, a time when "patterns of behavior are laid down, when environmental stimuli of all sorts must be integrated into a workable sense of self, when sensuality is being defined and fears elaborated, when pleasure confronts security and impulse encounters control".... In short, adolescence is a time of discovery and experience. The vulnerability of so significant a segment of our society during such a sensitive period of its development imposes a responsibility upon the State to assure that what should be a normal and natural experience does not for the unprepared become a *raison de regretter*, physically or emotionally....

Likewise, the statute here challenged serves a significant State interest, although many people, particularly those within the reach of its protection, may view it as an unwarranted infringement upon private life-styles. Social legislation hardly ever pleases everyone. We merely state that the justification of the statutory rape law rests not on a morality to which not all of our citizens may subscribe, but rather on the premise that physical and psychic injury can be the result when the members of the class sought to be protected engage in acts, the consequences of which they may neither perceive nor appreciate.

Defendant's other argument, that his due process rights were violated because subdivision 2 of section 130.25 of the Penal Law does not allow ignorance, fraud or mistake as a defense, ignores an established principle of law that "public policy may require that in the prohibition or punishment of particular acts it may be provided that he who shall do them shall do them at his peril and will not be heard to plead in defense good faith or ignorance...." This public policy is often demonstrated "in the exercise of what is called the police power where the emphasis of the statute is evidently upon achievement of some social betterment rather than the punishment of the crimes as in cases of *mala in se....*" We find no infirmity in a statute which, in the State's exercise of the police power, forbids 21-year-old males from having intercourse with females under 17, regardless of whether the accused is aware of the female's age.

Sandstrom v Montana (442 U.S. 510), upon which the dissent relies in urging reversal, is inapposite. There, the Supreme Court had before it a murder statute in which intent was a specific element of the crime. In Sandstrom ... a charge that "the law presumes that a person intends the ordinary consequences of his voluntary acts," was found defective because it impermissibly shifted the burden of proving intent, and freed the State from the duty to prove "'every fact necessary to constitute the crime * * * charged....'" Here, neither the statute in question nor any judicial instruction shifted the burden of proof. *Mens rea* is simply not an element of New York's statutory rape statute.

Accordingly, the judgment ... convicting defendant, upon his plea of guilty, of rape in the third degree and sentencing him to five years' probation, should be affirmed.

MULTIPLE CHOICE QUESTIONS

1. The court in People v. Newton held that the defendant committed:
    A. A crime.
    B. A voluntary act.
    C. Possession of a firearm.
    D. None of the above.

2. In People v. Newton, the court concluded:
    A. That Newton should be held for trial.
    B. That Newton should be released.
    C. That Newton should be convicted.
    D. None of the above.

3. In New York, depraved indifference is a component of what element?
    A. *Actus reus*.
    B. *Mens rea*.
    C. Causation.
    D. Result.

4. A strict liability crime has:
    A. Only one element.
    B. One *mens rea* element.
    C. No elements.
    D. No *mens rea* element.

5. The key element in determining sentences is:
    A. *Actus reus*.
    B. *Mens rea*.
    C. Causation.
    D. Result.

6. In People v. Strong, the court found that:
    A. The evidence showed that the act was either reckless or criminally negligent.
    B. The defendant acted in good faith and so was not criminally responsible.
    C. The evidence showed that the act could not have been criminally negligent.
    D. There was no *mens rea*.

DISCUSSION EXERCISES

1. In People v. Newton, what was the *actus reus* that was the focus of the case? Does the judge put form over substance in ruling that the defendant did not possess a gun he held? Today, would appellate courts reach the same decision? Should the defendant, Newton, be responsible for the possession of his gun in any place his plane landed?

2. What would be some human actions that would not be "voluntary" actions?

3. In the homicide illustrations above, could you make any arguments to show that the negligent and reckless killers were as morally culpable as the other killers?

4. What would be illustrations of knowing, reckless, and negligent killings?

5. For one week, read every issue of a newspaper that is published in a large city. Pick out five criminal cases and determine with what mental state the prosecution is alleging the defendant to have acted.

6. In People v. Dozier, why should the defendant be convicted of the crime of rape, even if he was clearly misled into believing that the girl was an adult?

Chapter Four

Parties to Crime: Complicity and Vicarious Liability

Introduction

In some circumstances, the criminal law makes one person responsible for the actions of another person. For instance, assume that defendants A and B intend for a victim to die. If A buys a gun, the murder weapon, and gives the gun to B with the intent that B use the gun to kill the victim, which B does, then A is as guilty of murder as is B. In characterizing defendant A, law enforcement personnel might refer to A as an "accessory," a "party to the crime," or an "accomplice." These characterizations are not crimes themselves. Rather, in New York, they represent the concept that one defendant, such as A, can be criminally responsible for the actions of another defendant, such as B, if both A and B commit an act that furthers their intent (to kill a person, as in the illustration above). For example, because A assisted B in intentionally causing the death of the victim, then A is as legally responsible as B for the death of the victim. Both A and B would be guilty of murder. Specifically, in New York, this concept is called "criminal liability for the conduct of another" (Penal Law 20.00).

Parties to Crime or Accessorial Liability

In the case below, People v. Comfort, consider what each brother was thinking (that is, their mental states) at the exact time that the police officer was killed.

People v. Comfort, 113 A.D.2d 420, 496 N.Y.S.2d 857 (4th Department 1985)

On the night of December 5, 1980 the defendant Joseph Comfort shot to death undercover New York State Police Investigator Robert Van Hall and grievously wounded his partner, William Gorenflo. This incident was the culmination of events which began on November 14, 1980 with the arrival in Corning, New York, of Jose Otero and Edwardo Blanco from Florida with 28 ounces of cocaine. The drugs were delivered to the defendant Larry Comfort who accepted them on assignment for sale and distribution in the Corning area and for which he agreed to pay $2,000 per ounce when the drugs were sold. Thereafter, Larry attempted to distribute and sell the cocaine. On November 28, 1980, Otero and Blanco returned to Corning in an effort to secure payment for the drugs and Larry eventually paid them approximately $10,750.

Trial testimony reflected that Larry had neither the remaining $46,000 which he owed them nor the bulk of the cocaine and that when Otero and Blanco pressed their demands upon him either to pay for the cocaine or return it to them, he became frightened and confused and expressed fears for his safety and that of his young son. After the partial payment was made Otero and Blanco were arrested at about 2:30 on the morning of December 5 by the New York State Police who seized the money, a small quantity of cocaine and a gun. At the instance of State Police investigators, Otero and Blanco contacted Larry on December 5 and attempted to arrange for the return of the balance of the cocaine. Larry in turn later enlisted the aid of his brother Joseph who obtained the concealed cocaine which remained and in a clandestine manner returned it to Otero and Blanco in the early evening of December 5. These events were monitored by the State Police who determined to arrest Larry on drug charges.

Following the transfer, Larry and Joseph returned to the home of Camille Comfort, Larry's ex-wife. Troopers William Gorenflo and Robert Van Hall, who were working undercover in an unmarked Plymouth automobile, placed the home of Camille Comfort, where the red Monte Carlo Chevrolet reportedly used in the drug transfer was parked, under surveillance in an effort to apprehend Larry Comfort. The Comforts observed the surveillance and feared that they were being followed by cohorts of Otero and Blanco. Larry left the house on foot and determined that he was being followed by the unidentified men. He eluded the undercover officers and when he returned a short time later to Camille Comfort's house, he told Joseph to "Grab the gun and come with me * * * the Cubans are going to kill me." Earlier in the day Larry had asked Joseph to get his shotgun and put it in the car they were then using.

The defendants then left in the Monte Carlo and drove around to try to identify the occupants of the Plymouth. Larry drove the car and Joseph was in the back seat with the shotgun. After the officers observed that the Monte Carlo was gone from the house, they left the area but soon observed behind them the car containing the defendants. As the Comforts accelerated and passed the officers' unmarked Plymouth, Joseph told Larry that he observed a "hippie kid" driving the car and an "old man" in the car. It is not disputed that the Plymouth followed in pursuit, that both cars drove through a "stop sign" and that the defendants' Monte Carlo turned into a lighted car wash, came to a stop, and was immediately rammed on the driver's side by the Plymouth. The two vehicles came to rest side by side. Joseph testified that as Larry yelled "Hold on, they're going to ram us," he placed two deer slugs into the shotgun.

After the collision Joseph observed the two men in the Plymouth, heard Larry shout "Run, they're going to kill us," and he then fired the shotgun. The bullet pierced the side window of the Plymouth, struck and killed Van Hall, who was seated in the passenger seat, passed through his body and struck Gorenflo in the back. Using his vehicle as cover Gorenflo fired two shots at Larry and Joseph as they ran; however, Joseph reached the corner of the car wash and Larry vanished into the darkness. Within a minute Joseph shot and grievously wounded Gorenflo.

The six-count single indictment charged that the defendants "intentionally aiding and being aided by each other" murdered Van Hall and attempted to murder Gorenflo. After an extensive trial the jury found both defendants guilty of murder in the second degree of Robert L. Van Hall, guilty of attempted murder in the second degree of William Gorenflo and guilty of first degree sale and possession of a controlled substance.

The principal issues on appeal are based on the defendants' contentions that: (1) the verdicts convicting them of murder and attempted murder were against the weight of the evidence; (2) the trial court committed reversible error in charging the jury to evaluate their justification defense based on what an ordinary, prudent man would have done; and (3) their due process rights were violated when the court refused to order disclosure of the identity of an informant which prevented them from obtaining information relative to their duress defense on the drug charges.

Larry Comfort

Since this defendant did not fire any shot during the course of the incident, his convictions of murder and attempted murder in the second degree were necessarily predicated on a theory of accessorial liability (Penal Law 20.00). For both charges the prosecution must show his intent to cause death (Penal Law 20.00, 110.00, 125.25 [1]). A review of the record reveals that the People failed to introduce sufficient evidence to sustain the convictions.

From November 14 to December 5, Larry and the two men he referred to as the "Cubans" engaged in a cocaine enterprise operated in Corning. On the evening of the incident he planned to extricate himself from that drug scheme. After arranging to transfer the remaining cocaine to Otero and Blanco, Larry procured the services of the codefendant, his brother Joseph, to carry out the transaction. Following the drop-off, Larry told Joseph that he feared Otero and Blanco would kill him because he diluted the cocaine. When Larry reentered Camille's house upon ascertaining that the occupants of the Plymouth were following him, he instructed Joseph to "Grab the gun and come with me." As Larry drove alongside the Plymouth, Joseph informed him that it did not have Florida license plates and that its occupants were not Otero and Blanco. While Larry drove into the car wash area and stated "Hold on, they're going to ram us," Joseph loaded the shotgun. Subsequent to the collision but prior to any shooting, Larry yelled "Run, they're going to kill us" and exited the Monte Carlo.

Larry's behavior in insisting that they drive into the night armed with a shotgun does not establish beyond a reasonable doubt an intent to kill the Plymouth's occupants, nor was there any proof or an agreement or common design between the brothers to kill them. The record is consistent with a spontaneous, independent decision by Joseph to shoot the undercover officers). The defendants left Camille's house for the avowed purpose of discovering if Otero and Blanco were connected with the Plymouth. The act of driving around Corning with a shotgun is not inconsistent with that objective and does not prove an intent to hunt down and kill the investigators.

Moreover, Larry's subsequent conduct tends to disprove an inference of such intent. Rather than firing into the Plymouth while driving alongside it, Larry accelerated the Monte Carlo, drove ahead, and stopped in a well-lit area. An instant after impact Larry shouted "run" which could be interpreted as an exhortation for Joseph to escape from the area. At the time Joseph fired the initial shot every indication was that Larry was fleeing the scene. The logical inference was that Joseph formulated the intent to slay the

Plymouth's occupants subsequent to Larry's warning that the Plymouth was going to ram the Monte Carlo, since he placed two deer slugs into the shotgun at that point. Alternatively, it could be inferred that Joseph spontaneously resolved to slay the Plymouth's occupants after Larry issued a warning that the occupants were going to kill them and after he saw the occupants turn to exit the Plymouth. Either way, it may be considered to have been a spontaneously formed and independent intent on the part of Joseph.

Without adequate proof of shared intent with the principal actor, there is no basis for finding that Larry acted in concert with Joseph, the actual killer. In addition, where a defendant's conviction is based entirely upon circumstantial evidence, as here, the facts from which the inference of his guilt is drawn must exclude to a moral certainly every reasonable hypothesis of innocence. No proof was presented that excluded to a moral certainty the inference that Joseph spontaneously formed the decision to fire the gun or that Larry ever knew of his brother's intention to kill Van Hall and Gorenflo. In the absence of such proof Joseph's homicidal intent should not be imputed to Larry. Neither was there any evidence that demonstrated that Larry had a separate, specific intent to kill the investigators. As the inference of guilt is not the only one that can be fairly and reasonably drawn from the record, and since the evidence does not negate, beyond a reasonable doubt, every reasonable hypothesis of innocence the convictions for murder and attempted murder cannot be sustained.

The concept of accessorial liability can cover a broad range of activity. For example, until New York law was amended (Penal Law 130.35), the crime of rape was defined as an act by a male of forcible sexual intercourse with a female who was not the man's wife.

People v. Evans, 58 A.D.2d 919, 396 N.Y.S.2d 727 (3rd Department 1977)

Appeal from a judgment of the County Court of Albany County, rendered November 15, 1976, convicting defendant upon her plea of guilty of the crime of rape in the first degree. Defendant pleaded guilty to an accusation of rape in the first degree in satisfaction of an indictment charging her with that offense as well as the crimes of first degree sodomy, unlawful imprisonment and second degree assault. Her contention on appeal that she could not properly be convicted of that crime is wholly without merit. The indictment alleged that she and another had intentionally aided a male codefendant in having sexual intercourse with the female victim by forcible compulsion. Defendant admitted her participation in the incident before her guilty plea was accepted. Essentially, this involvement consisted of beating and holding the victim down while the male codefendant had intercourse with her. That being the case, defendant's liability for the conduct of her associates stands adequately established (Penal Law 20.00) and the fact that she is legally incapable of committing such an offense in her individual capacity has no effect on these proceedings.... Defendant was sentenced to an indeterminate period of imprisonment with a minimum term of 8 1/3 and a maximum term of 25 years…. Her remaining argument that the sentence was unduly harsh and excessive is, under the circumstances of this case, without merit…. Judgment affirmed.

Vicarious Liability

Vicarious liability is a concept that holds a defendant responsible for the acts of another person, even though the defendant did not share the mental state of the other person or commit any act that led to an undesirable result. Vicarious liability is different from accessorial liability (discussed above), where defendants must share the same mental state before they can be liable for the acts of each other. Vicarious liability is rare in the criminal law, but prosecutors sometimes use the concept to hold liable persons in authority in businesses or corporations (Penal Law 20.25).

The purpose of vicarious liability is to encourage persons in authority to exercise great care over the actions of their employees and enterprises, which may have unusual societal dangers and risks associated with them. For example, society may want to encourage drug makers, meat processors, and operators of nuclear generators to exercise extraordinary care over the work of their subordinates to ensure public safety. That is, when someone errs when handling inherently dangerous products, such as drugs, food, or nuclear energy, catastrophic results can occur. Thus, when a subordinate makes an error, the person in authority may be held criminally responsible for the act of the subordinate to encourage higher levels of care in conducting the business. The person in authority is thus "vicariously liable" for the conduct of another person.

In the Byrne case below, analyze the mental state of the defendant. Under what circumstances can the head of a business be held responsible for the actions of someone else connected to the business? In the Byrne case, consider whether the sale of alcohol is a business in which strict liability should exist.

People v. Byrne, 77 N.Y.2d 460, 570 N.E.2d 1066, 568 N.Y.S.2d 717 (1991)

[T]he Alcoholic Beverage Control Law prohibits the sale of alcoholic beverages to minors. It is well established that the crime created by these statutes is one of "strict liability" for which proof of the accused's guilty knowledge or intent is not required. The question presented on this appeal is whether these statutes also create a crime of "vicarious liability," permitting conviction of a natural person for the acts of another solely because of the parties' business relationship.

On March 12, 1983, Thomas Byrne, defendant James Byrne's brother, allegedly sold alcoholic beverages to two individuals who were under the age of 19. The alleged sales occurred in a Bronx County tavern known as Manions, which was owned by a

41

corporate entity called Tullow Taverns, Inc. Defendant and his brother Thomas each owned 50% of the shares of this corporation. Additionally, defendant held the title of corporate president, while Thomas was designated secretary-treasurer.

Defendant and Thomas Byrne were both charged with violating Alcoholic Beverage Control Law by "sell[ing] or caus[ing] or permit[ting] to be sold alcoholic beverages, to wit; beer to [a] person * * * being actually or apparently under the age of nineteen years." Following pretrial motions, the charges against defendant were dismissed because there were no "factual allegations that [defendant] was present in the tavern at the time the alcoholic beverages were served or that he had notice of or participated in such conduct." However, the Appellate Term reversed the dismissal order and reinstated the charges, holding that "the defendant, if adjudged a responsible officer of the corporate licensee, may be held criminally liable notwithstanding his lack of knowledge of, or participation in, the criminal act."

Defendant was subsequently tried before a jury. The evidence at his trial established only that defendant's brother Thomas had sold beer to two underage individuals on the premises of Manions, that defendant was a shareholder and officer of Manions' corporate owner and that defendant had previously assumed some managerial responsibilities. There was no proof that defendant was present during, or had any other connection with, the illicit sales for which he was charged. Nonetheless, the jury was instructed that it could find defendant guilty of violating Alcoholic Beverage Control Law if, in addition to determining that Thomas Byrne had made the sales in violation of the statute, the jury believed that defendant was a "responsible officer" of Tullow Taverns, Inc. Defendant was convicted and sentenced to pay a fine. Following his conviction, defendant appealed to the Appellate Term.

Since it is undisputed that defendant did not participate, encourage or know about the March 12, 1983 illicit sales, and, in fact, was not even present in Manions tavern when the sales occurred, he can have no criminal liability for those sales, unless Alcoholic Beverage Control Law 65 (1) and 130 (3) are construed to authorize the imposition of vicarious liability based solely upon defendant's status as a shareholder and "responsible" officer of Manions corporate owner.

[W]e begin our analysis with the specific language of the controlling Alcoholic Beverage Control Law provisions. Neither statute contains express language extending the legislatively imposed duty beyond the actor who actually engages in the prohibited conduct. Thus, if some form of vicarious liability is to be imposed, we must look elsewhere for a source of authority for doing so.

The People suggest that such a source of authority may be found in Alcoholic Beverage Control Law ... which defines the term "person" to include corporations and other business entities, thereby authorizing the imposition of derivative liability, at least in one circumstance. However, the legislatively conferred authority to prosecute corporations for Alcoholic Beverage Control Law violations is quite specific and does not support the inference that the Legislature intended to effect a much broader rule of general vicarious liability for all criminal prosecutions under the Alcoholic Beverage Control Law, including those against natural persons.

Furthermore, any attempted analogy between the criminal liability of corporations and that of individuals falters because of the essential differences in the underlying theories supporting the imposition of derivative liability. It is true that when a corporation is prosecuted, the factual predicate for its liability is, invariably, the conduct of someone else, namely its agents or employees. However, since corporations, which are legal fictions, can operate only through their designated agents and employees (see, e.g., United States v. Dotterweich, 320 U.S. 277, 281), the acts of the latter are, in a sense, the acts of the corporation as well. Thus, when a corporation is held criminally liable because it is a "person" under Alcoholic Beverage Control Law, it is, in reality, being made to answer for its own acts. Such a theory of liability is a far cry from one involving true vicarious liability, in which, by virtue of the parties' relationship, the conduct of one individual is artificially imputed to another who "has played no part in it [and] has done nothing whatever to aid or encourage it."

Equally unpersuasive is the People's attempt to extrapolate a legislative intention to impose vicarious liability from the fact that the statutes at issue create a strict liability crime. A crime of strict liability is one that does not require proof of a culpable mental state (Penal Law 15.10). The doctrine of vicarious liability, in contrast, eliminates the need to prove that the accused personally committed the forbidden act. Since the concepts are distinct, there is no reason to infer that a Legislature willing to adopt the former would also endorse the latter. Indeed, in the absence of a specific expression to the contrary, a legislative intention to impose criminal liability where the actual actor did not harbor a guilty state of mind and the person to be held liable did not participate in the proscribed conduct cannot sensibly be assumed.

Finally, where the Legislature has not clearly directed otherwise, we should be most reluctant to embrace the doctrine of vicarious liability for use in the criminal sphere. The doctrine runs counter to the generally accepted premise in the criminal law that individuals "'must * * * answer for their own acts, and stand or fall by their own behaviour'." Further, it is out of harmony with several provisions of the Penal Law, which are instructive on the Legislature's over-all attitude toward individual responsibility.

In closing, we stress that our decision in this case does not represent a policy-based rejection of the use of vicarious liability theories in criminal prosecutions. The fairness and wisdom of imposing such liability are matters within the purview of the Legislature's judgment, provided, of course, that the constraints of due process are observed. We merely hold here that in the face of legislative silence on the point, a legislative intent to authorize prosecution for another's criminal conduct will not be inferred.

Accordingly, the order of the Appellate Term should be reversed and the complaint dismissed. Order reversed.

MULTIPLE CHOICE QUESTIONS

1. Which of the following are crimes?
   A. Complicity.
   B. Vicarious liability.
   C. Robbery.
   D. All the above.

2. In the Comfort case, what best describes the court's conclusion with regard to the defendant Larry Comfort?
   A. The defendant was an accomplice.
   B. The defendant was vicariously liable.
   C. The defendant was a party to a crime.
   D. None of the above.

3. What best describes one of the court's conclusions from the Byrne case?
   A. The defendant was an accomplice.
   B. The defendant was vicariously liable.
   C. The defendant was a party to a crime.
   D. None of the above.

4. Vicarious liability is usually limited to:
   A. *Mala in se* crimes.
   B. *Malum prohibitum* crimes.
   C. Any crime.
   D. None of the above.

5. In New York, one person can be responsible for the actions of another person under the theory of:
   A. Complicity.
   B. Vicarious liability.
   C. Parties to crime.
   D. All the above.

DISCUSSION EXERCISES

1. Explain the differences between complicity and vicarious liability. What would be an example of vicarious liability in civil law?

2. What would have been the mental state of a defendant who is found to be guilty of a crime on a theory of complicity?

3. Discuss the policy reasons for holding a person responsible for an act that he or she did not commit. Or for which he or she did not know about.

4. What would be an argument for not holding persons vicariously liable for the *mala in se* crimes of other persons?

5. Discuss why you do or do not agree with the holdings in the cases above.

6. Could there be any circumstances under which a woman could be convicted of rape?

7. In People v. Comfort, do you believe that either defendant was legally or morally responsible for the death of the police officer? Even if the defendants, who were brothers, did not know that the men chasing them were police officers, did they recklessly cause the death of the officers?

8. If one engages in drug dealing, does he not accept the risk that someone may die, either from the use of drugs or from the violence associated with the drug trade?

Chapter Five

Uncompleted Crimes: Conspiracy, Attempt, and Solicitation

Introduction

Attempt, conspiracy, and solicitation are crimes that consist of actions and planning that are designed to bring about a certain result, which in itself is a crime. They are sometimes called "inchoate" or "unfinished" crimes, but such a characterization can be a misnomer, because they are actually crimes themselves. That is, even if defendants do not achieve their underlying intent of robbing a bank, for example, they can be found guilty of attempting or conspiring to rob a bank or soliciting another person to rob a bank.

Conspiracy

A conspiracy is committed when any person agrees with one or more other persons to engage in conduct that is designed to result in the commission of another crime (Penal Law 105.00). The conduct or actions of the conspirators might be completely legal. For example, three persons may be playing cards one night and decide that they would like to play for higher stakes in future card games, but they need more money. They agree to rob a bank and apportion their responsibility as follows: defendant A will buy a car to use during the escape; defendant B will buy a kitchen knife to use to coerce the bank teller to relinquish the money; and defendant C will buy Halloween masks to conceal their identities.

Standing alone, the actions of A, B, and C (buying a car, a knife, and masks) would be legal in every respect, except that the actions are bound by the defendants' intent to commit an underlying crime—the robbery. In New York, the defendants would be guilty of conspiracy. The elements of conspiracy are the: (1) intent to commit an underlying crime, (2) agreement of two or more persons to commit the underlying crime, and (3) commission of an act that is designed to further the conspiracy (Penal Law 105.20), such as buying the mask to use in the robbery, which should be referred to as an "overt act." The following case discusses the element of an agreement to commit the underlying crime.

People v. Caban, 772 N.Y.S.2d 675 (1st Department 2004)

Judgment, Supreme Court, Bronx County (John Moore, J.), rendered December 22, 1997, convicting defendant, after a jury trial, of conspiracy in the second degree, and sentencing him to a term of 8 1/3 to 25 years, affirmed.

Saxe and Gonzalez, JJ. concur in a memorandum by Gonzalez, J. as follows:

In this prosecution of defendant for conspiring with others to murder a rival drug dealer, there are two primary issues on appeal. The first is whether the prosecution established a *prima facie* case of conspiracy by evidence independent of the hearsay declarations of two coconspirators sought to be introduced at trial....

In March 1995, prosecution witness George Castro was a street-level drug dealer working for defendant Carlos Caban's drug business on Fox Street, between 156th Street and Longwood Avenue, in the Bronx. Angel Ortiz, a rival drug dealer, also sold crack on Fox Street.

At defendant's trial, Castro testified that on March 18, 1995, he was packaging crack for sale at a "stash house" located in apartment 4A at 777 Fox Street. Also present were defendant and his brother, Derrick Garcia, and at least two other drug sellers, Pello Torres and Melvin Butler. According to Castro, defendant announced that Ortiz "needed to be killed" because he was taking business away from him. Defendant offered to pay $ 5,000 for the murder, to which Garcia responded "I'll do it." Torres then stated that he would provide a gun.

On cross-examination, Castro admitted that one day in mid-March 1995, he, Torres and Butler went to the corner of 156th and Fox Street, planning to kill Ortiz. Butler was armed with two guns and Castro acted as a look-out. However, the plan was aborted when the police arrived on the scene.

On June 1, 1995, at approximately 8:50 P.M., Ortiz was in a playground on Fox Street with his girlfriend's four-year-old daughter and three of his dealers. At about 9:00 P.M., as Castro stood in front of 777 Fox Street, Torres approached him from the direction of 156th Street and said "It's time." Torres then entered 777 Fox Street, and shortly thereafter, Garcia exited the building with another man. Castro followed Garcia and the second man to the playground; Castro stopped across the street in front of 725 Fox Street. From there, Castro observed Garcia walk over to Ortiz and begin arguing with him over defendant's drug "spot." As Ortiz tried to walk away, Garcia shot him multiple times "real close to his back," resulting in Ortiz's death.

On November 8, 1995, Castro was arrested for two drug sales. Realizing that he was "facing a lot of time," he told a homicide detective that he had information about two homicides, including the Ortiz murder. Castro ultimately entered into a cooperation agreement with the Bronx District Attorney's Office whereby he was permitted to plead guilty to a misdemeanor and receive a sentence of three years' probation in exchange for his testimony against defendant.

During defendant's trial, defense counsel objected to the admission of Garcia's statement "I'll do it," and Torres's statements that he would procure the gun and "It's time," on hearsay grounds. The trial court admitted the statements conditionally, subject to the prosecution's establishing a *prima facie* case of conspiracy without recourse to those statements.

On appeal, defendant argues that the trial court erred in admitting, over his objection, the hearsay declarations of Garcia and Torres because the People failed to establish a *prima facie* case of conspiracy without recourse to those declarations. He contends that without the hearsay evidence, there is no evidence of an agreement to kill Ortiz and therefore the evidence was legally insufficient to establish his guilt of conspiracy. We disagree....

A *prima facie* case of conspiracy requires evidence "that a person, with intent that conduct constituting a crime be performed, agrees with one or more persons to engage or cause the performance of such conduct…. Defendant argues that stripped of the hearsay, the trial evidence merely established that defendant wanted Ortiz killed, that he offered $ 5,000 to Garcia and others to have him killed and that three months later Garcia killed Ortiz…. [D]efendant argues that this evidence did not establish a *prima facie* agreement between defendant, Garcia and Torres to kill Ortiz. [Note: Defendant makes no argument that the People failed to make a *prima facie* showing of the "overt act" element of the crime of conspiracy].

The circumstantial proof of an agreement is … sufficient to establish a prima face case of conspiracy to murder Ortiz…. [H]ere there are admissions from defendant's own mouth establishing that he offered to pay $ 5,000 for the murder of Ortiz to any one of several associates present at the March 18 meeting. This evidence provided a clear nexus linking defendant to Ortiz's murder. Additional evidence showed that in June 1995, Torres went into the building where defendant's stash house was located, Garcia exited shortly thereafter and Garcia walked directly to the park where Ortiz was located. Garcia argued with Ortiz about defendant's drug "spot" and then shot him.

Although defendant argues that there was never any admissible evidence establishing that Garcia or Torres accepted defendant's offer to murder Ortiz for $ 5,000, overwhelming circumstantial evidence demonstrates just the opposite. Defendant's own words establish a clear economic motive to have Ortiz killed. In addition, Garcia's and Torres's relationship to defendant as dealers in his drug business provide the strongest inference that they were acting on behalf of defendant…. Additionally, since the murder was committed by one of the persons who attended the March 18 meeting (Garcia), with the possible involvement of two others who attended the same meeting (Torres and Castro), the conclusion is inescapable that Ortiz's murder was the direct result of defendant's March 18 offer. Moreover, the fact that Garcia murdered Ortiz immediately after arguing with him over defendant's drug spot is also powerful, confirmatory evidence of the March 18 agreement.

Because the crucial evidence of defendant's membership in the conspiracy is established by his own admissions … and because strong circumstantial proof demonstrates that defendant's offer to pay $ 5,000 to murder Ortiz was accepted by one or more of his associates, the prosecution established a prima face case of conspiracy by independent evidence justifying admission of the coconspirators' statements….

Attempt

An "attempt" to commit a crime is itself a crime, even though the intended crime never occurs. An attempt to commit a crime is complete when a defendant "engages in conduct which tends to effect the commission of such crime" (Penal Law 110.00). The concept of what is an attempted crime is relatively clear; a defendant does something to cause the result he or she is seeking, such as in the Arroyo case, above, where one of the defendants tried to kill the delivery man. Because the victim was not killed, the defendant was guilty of an "attempted murder." Had the intended victim been killed, the defendant (and his co-conspirators) would have been guilty of murder, not attempted murder.

However, it can sometimes be difficult to determine what action of the defendant "tends to effect the crime." For example, if a defendant buys a gun with the intent of killing the victim later in the day, has the defendant's action tended to effect, or cause, the crime? Should the defendant be guilty of attempted murder? If the defendant aims his gun at the victim but is struck by a bolt of lightening just before he pulls the trigger, is the defendant guilty of an attempt to commit murder? Often, people become angry and think, "I hope he dies." They buy a gun with the intent to kill someone the next day. However, when the next day arrives, they have a change of heart and decide not to kill someone. Can the person still be charged with an attempted murder because he bought a gun yesterday with which to commit a killing?

In the Rizzo case that follows, consider what principle you can use to decide how to determine whether defendants should be guilty of an attempted crime.

People v. Rizzo, 246 N.Y. 334, 158 N.E. 888, 55 A.L.R. 711 (1927)

The police of the city of New York did excellent work in this case by preventing the commission of a serious crime. It is a great satisfaction to realize that we have such wide-awake guardians of our peace. Whether or not the steps which the defendant had taken up to the time of his arrest amounted to the commission of a crime, as defined by our law, is, however, another matter. He has been convicted of an attempt to commit the crime of robbery in the first degree and sentenced to State's prison. There is no doubt that he had the intention to commit robbery if he got the chance. An examination, however, of the facts is necessary to determine whether his acts were in preparation to commit the crime if the opportunity offered, or constituted a crime in itself, known to our law as an attempt to commit robbery in the first degree.

Charles Rizzo, the defendant, appellant, with three others, Anthony J. Dorio, Thomas Milo and John Thomasello, on January 14th planned to rob one Charles Rao of a payroll valued at about $ 1,200 which he was to carry from the bank for the United Lathing Company. These defendants, two of whom had firearms, started out in an automobile, looking for Rao or the man who had the payroll on that day. Rizzo claimed to be able to identify the man and was to point him out to the others who were to do the actual holding up. The four rode about in their car looking for Rao. They went to the bank from which he was supposed to get the money and to various buildings being constructed by the United Lathing Company. At last they came to One Hundred and Eightieth street and Morris Park avenue [sic].

By this time they were watched and followed by two police officers. As Rizzo jumped out of the car and ran into the building all four were arrested. The defendant was taken out from the building in which he was hiding. Neither Rao nor a man named Previti, who was also supposed to carry a payroll, were at the place at the time of the arrest. The defendants had not found or seen the man they intended to rob; no person with a payroll was at any of the places where they had stopped and no one had been pointed out or identified by Rizzo. The four men intended to rob the payroll man, whoever he was; they were looking for him, but they had not seen or discovered him up to the time they were arrested.

Does this constitute the crime of an attempt to commit robbery in the first degree? The Penal Law [since amended] prescribes "An act, done with intent to commit a crime, and tending but failing to effect its commission, is 'an attempt to commit that crime.'" The word "tending" is very indefinite. It is perfectly evident that there will arise differences of opinion as to whether an act in a given case is one tending to commit a crime. "Tending" means to exert activity in a particular direction. Any act in preparation to commit a crime may be said to have a tendency towards its accomplishment. The procuring of the automobile… [and] searching the streets looking for the desired victim…were in reality acts tending toward the commission of the proposed crime.

The law, however, has recognized that many acts in the way of preparation are too remote to constitute the crime of attempt. The line has been drawn between those acts which are remote and those which are proximate and near to the consummation. The law must be practical, and, therefore, considers those acts only as tending to the commission of the crime which are so near to its accomplishment that in all reasonable probability the crime itself would have been committed but for timely interference. The cases which have been before the courts express this idea in different language, but the idea remains the same. The act or acts must come or advance very near to the accomplishment of the intended crime. In People v. Mills (178 N. Y. 274, 284) it was said: "Felonious intent alone is not enough, but there must be an overt act shown in order to establish even an attempt. An overt act is one done to carry out the intention, and it must be such as would naturally effect that result, unless prevented by some extraneous cause." In Hyde v. U. S. (225 U.S. 347) it was stated that the act amounts to an attempt when it is so near to the result that the danger of success is very great. "There must be dangerous proximity to success." Halsbury in his "Laws of England" (Vol. IX, p. 259) says: "An act, in order to be a criminal attempt, must be immediately, and not remotely, connected with and directly tending to the commission of an offence."

As I have said before, minds differ over proximity and the nearness of the approach. How shall we apply this rule of immediate nearness to this case? The defendants were looking for the payroll man to rob him of his money. This is the charge in the indictment…. To constitute the crime of robbery the money must have been taken from Rao by means of force or violence, or through fear. The crime of attempt to commit robbery was committed if these defendants did an act tending to the commission of this robbery. Did the acts above describe come dangerously near to the taking of Rao's property? Did the acts come so near the commission of robbery that there was reasonable likelihood of its accomplishment but for the interference? Rao was not found; the defendants were still looking for him; no attempt to rob him could be made, at least until he came in sight; he was not in the building at One Hundred and Eightieth street and

Morris Park avenue. There was no man there with the payroll for the United Lathing Company whom these defendants could rob. Apparently no money had been drawn from the bank for the payroll by anybody at the time of the arrest. In a word, these defendants had planned to commit a crime and were looking around the city for an opportunity to commit it, but the opportunity fortunately never came. Men would not be guilty of an attempt at burglary if they had planned to break into a building and were arrested while they were hunting about the streets for the building not knowing where it was. Neither would a man be guilty of an attempt to commit murder if he armed himself and started out to find the person whom he had planned to kill but could not find him. So here these defendants were not guilty of an attempt to commit robbery in the first degree when they had not found or reached the presence of the person they intended to rob. For these reasons, the judgment of conviction of this defendant, appellant, must be reversed and a new trial granted.

Sometimes the crimes of attempt and conspiracy can appear in the same case. This may give rise to issues about the appropriate sentence. Consider the Arroyo case, below, in which the court distinguishes the crimes of attempted murder and conspiracy to commit murder. Use the Arroyo case to examine how the crimes of conspiracy and attempted murder are analyzed in New York. Note how the court finds that conspiracy and attempted murder have different elements. They are thus separate crimes. Therefore, for each crime, a judge may impose different and consecutive sentences instead of imposing sentences that can be served at the same time ("concurrent sentences").

People v. Arroyo, 93 N.Y.2d 990, 717 N.E.2d 696, 695 N.Y.S.2d 537 (1999)

In January 1991, after some discussion and planning, defendant[s], Jose Sorrentini [sic] [Arroyo was not noted in the court's opinion, but presumably he was the driver or the lookout;] and Chris Claudio--the driver, the lookout and the shooter, respectively--lured Guy Maresca to a deserted area in the Bronx by ordering pizza from his place of employment. When Maresca drove to the appointed address to make his delivery, Claudio ran toward him and fired a single shot. He missed. Claudio made a second attempt to shoot Maresca, but the gun jammed and Maresca sped away. Based on information provided by Sorrentini, a police informant, all three men were arrested and charged. After trial, defendant was convicted of conspiracy in the second degree, attempted murder in the second degree and criminal possession of a weapon in the second degree. He was sentenced to consecutive, indeterminate prison terms of 8 1/3 to 25 years and 5 to 15 years, respectively, on the attempted murder and conspiracy counts and to a concurrent term of 5 to 15 years on the weapons possession count.

On appeal, defendant asserts that the court was without authority to impose consecutive sentences for conspiracy and attempted murder. We disagree.

Concurrent sentences are required only "for two or more offenses committed through a single act or omission, or through an act or omission which in itself constituted one of the offenses and also was a material element of the other" (Penal Law 70.25 [2]). Thus, consecutive sentences may not be imposed "(1) where a single act constitutes two offenses, or (2) where a single act constitutes one of the offenses and a material element of the other."

To establish the defendant's guilt of conspiracy in the second degree, the People were required to prove that, with the intent that a class A felony be committed, the defendant agreed with others to engage in or cause the felony to be committed (Penal Law 105.15) and that one of the conspirators committed an overt act in furtherance of the criminal scheme (Penal Law 105.20). On the other hand, an attempt to commit murder in the second degree required proof that, with the intent to commit the crime of murder in the second degree, the defendant engaged in conduct which tended to effect the commission of that crime (Penal Law 110.00, 125.25 [1]).

While there might be a statutory overlap in the definition of these crimes, in this case the People established the commission of separate and distinct acts supporting the imposition of consecutive sentences. When defendant, Claudio and Sorrentini met on the evening of January 8, 1991, armed and prepared to seek out Maresca, the crime of conspiracy was complete. The conspiracy statute does not specify any particular conduct to satisfy the requirement that there be an overt act in furtherance of the conspiracy. Indeed, we have previously stated that "the function of the overt act in a conspiracy prosecution is 'simply to manifest "that the conspiracy is at work" ....' The overt act must be an independent act that tends to carry out the conspiracy, but need not necessarily be the object of the crime" (People v Ribowsky, 77 NY2d 284, 293). Approximately one hour after they met, the conspirators saw Maresca, shot at him, missed and attempted to shoot again. These separate and distinct acts constituted the crime of attempted murder in the second degree. Order affirmed in a memorandum.

Solicitation

In New York, a person is guilty of criminal solicitation when he or she "solicits, requests, commands, importunes, or otherwise attempts to cause" another person to commit an underlying crime. A classic illustration of solicitation occurs when a defendant offers a "hitman" money to kill the defendant's spouse. The defendant's mere request constitutes the crime of solicitation, the elements of which are: (1) the intent that another person commit a crime and (2) a request of another person that he or she commit the crime. The crime of solicitation relieves law enforcement personnel of the burden of having to wait until the hitman engages in an act of preparation for the crime (which increases the risk that the intended crime will occur) before making an arrest.

Use the Lubow case, below, to determine the public policy implications behind the application of the solicitation statute. Is it possible that someone might be convicted for solicitation without an intent that someone really carry out the crime he requests? For example, assume that a husband and a wife have a fight and the husband tells his best friend, "I'd have my life back if my wife were dead." Is the husband asking his best friend to kill is wife? Does solicitation allow convictions where the husband was only "sounding off?" Should solicitation be eliminated as a crime because it requires so little evidence for conviction (a request that someone commit a crime, with the inference that the requester really wants the crime committed)? Would it be socially beneficial to repeal solicitation statutes and simply charge people with conspiracy, which requires that either the husband in the example above, or his confederate, commit an overt act? By requiring additional proof (the occurrence of an overt act), would this scheme prevent solicitation convictions of persons who really had no intent that a crime occur even though their words suggested they did want someone to commit a crime on their behalf? In the Lubow case, consider whether the defendant really wanted someone else to commit the crime of grand larceny.

People v. Lubow, 29 N.Y.2d 58, 272 N.E.2d 331, 323 N.Y.S.2d 829 (1971)

Appellants have been convicted after a trial by a three-Judge panel in the Criminal Court of the City of New York of violation of section 100.05. The information on which the prosecution is based is made by complainant Max Silverman. It describes the charge as criminal solicitation and states that "defendants attempted to cause deponent to commit the crime of grand larceny" in that they "attempted to induce the deponent to obtain precious stones on partial credit with a view towards appropriating the property to their own use and not paying the creditors, said conduct constituting the crime of larceny by false promise."

The evidence showed that complainant Silverman and both defendants were engaged in the jewelry business. It could be found that defendant Lubow owed Silverman $ 30,000 for diamonds on notes which were unpaid; that Lubow had told Silverman he was associated with a big operator interested in buying diamonds and introduced him to defendant Gissinger. It could also be found that in October, 1967, Silverman met the two defendants together at their office, demanded his money, and said that because of the amount owed him he was being forced into bankruptcy.

Silverman testified in response to this Lubow said "Well, let's make it a big one, a big bankruptcy," and Gissinger said this was a good idea. When Silverman asked "how it is done" he testified that Lubow, with Gissinger participating, outlined a method by which diamonds would be purchased partly on credit, sold for less than cost, with the proceeds pyramided to boost Silverman's credit rating until very substantial amounts came in, when there was to be a bankruptcy with Silverman explaining that he had lost the cash gambling in Puerto Rico and Las Vegas. The cash would be divided among the three men. The gambling explanation for the disappearance of cash would be made to seem believable by producing credit cards for Puerto Rico and Las Vegas. Silverman testified that Lubow said "we would eventually wind up with a quarter of a million dollars each" and that Gissinger said "maybe millions."

Silverman reported this proposal to the District Attorney in October, 1967 and the following month a police detective equipped Silverman with a tape recorder concealed on his person which was in operation during conversations with defendants on November 16 and which tends to substantiate the charge. The reel was received in evidence on concession that it was taken from the machine Silverman wore November 16.

A police detective testified as an expert that a "bust out operation" is a "pyramiding of credit by rapid purchasing of merchandise, and the rapid selling of the same merchandise sometimes 10 and 20 per cent the cost of the merchandise itself, and they keep selling and buying until they establish such a credit rating that they are able to purchase a large order at the end of their operation, and at this time they go into bankruptcy or they just leave."

There thus seems sufficient evidence in the record to find that defendants intended Silverman to engage in conduct constituting a felony by defrauding creditors of amounts making out grand larceny and that they importuned Silverman to engage in such conduct. Thus the proof meets the actual terms of the statute.

There are, however, potential difficulties inherent in this penal provision which should be looked at, even though all of them are not decisive in this present case. One, of course, is the absence of any need for corroboration. The tape recording here tends to give some independent support to the testimony of Silverman, but there are types of criminal conduct which might be solicited where there would be a heavy thrust placed on the credibility of a single witness testifying to a conversation. Extraordinary care might be required in deciding when to prosecute; in determining the truth; and in appellate review of the factual decision.

One example would be the suggestion of one person to another that he commit a sexual offense; another is the suggestion that he commit perjury. The Model Penal Code did not require corroboration; but aside from the need for corroboration which is traditional in some sexual offenses, there are dangers in the misinterpretation of innuendos or remarks which could be taken as invitations to commit sexual offenses.

The basic public justification for legislative enactment is, however, very similar to New York's and was developed in the Burt opinion: "Legislative concern with the proscribed soliciting is demonstrated not only by the gravity of the crimes specified but by the fact that the crime, unlike conspiracy, does not require the commission of any overt act. It is complete when the solicitation is made, and it is immaterial that the object of the solicitation is never consummated, or that no steps are taken toward its consummation." Another potential problem with the statute is that it includes an attempt to commit unlawful solicitation, i.e., solicits, etc., "or otherwise attempts to cause" the conduct. This could be an attempt in the classic sense and might be committed by a telephone message initiated but never delivered. The present Penal Law, stated in different language, has the same effect. [Despite its concerns, the court affirmed the judgment of conviction.]

MULTIPLE CHOICE QUESTIONS

1. What is the *mens rea* in inchoate crimes?
    - A. Intent.
    - B. Recklessness.
    - C. Negligence.
    - D. All the above.

2. What is the rule from the Rizzo case with regard to determining attempt?
    - A. The act must come very near to the accomplished crime.
    - B. An overt act will suffice for conviction if it is near in time to the crime.
    - C. The person attempting the crime must exhibit the mental state of negligence.
    - D. All the above.

3. In New York, based on the Arroyo case, a defendant can be convicted of only one inchoate crime?
    - A. True.
    - B. False.

4. In New York, based on the Arroyo case, a defendant can be sentenced for only either an inchoate crime or the underlying crime?
    - A. True.
    - B. False.

5. What is one of the dangers to defendants and citizens with regard to the proof needed to prove solicitation?
    - A. The proof does not need to establish guilt beyond a reasonable doubt.
    - B. The proof does not require corroboration.
    - C. The defendant has the burden of disproving solicitation.
    - D. All the above.

DISCUSSION EXERCISES

1. Discuss what evidence a prosecutor could rely on to prove conspiracy, attempt, and solicitation.

2. How could an "innocent" comment be construed as an element of solicitation or conspiracy?

3. If you were a prosecutor, what evidence would you require before prosecuting a defendant for solicitation?

4. If a person solicits a hit man to kill the person's spouse but then tells the hit man not to commit the killing, should the person be guilty of solicitation?

5. What would be a reason to require that an overt act be an element of solicitation?

6. Can we create language that is precise enough to tell citizens exactly when their actions become an attempt to commit a crime? For example, does the well-used phrase "beyond mere preparation" tell when conduct becomes an attempt? If language cannot be made more precise, is not the definition of what is an attempt to commit a crime really just a policy determination, or a "gut feeling," that some action constitutes a crime?

7. In People v. Rizzo, the Court go too far? Did Rizzo attempt to commit a crime, or is he innocent?

Chapter Six

Defenses to Criminal Liability: Justifications

Introduction

Every defendant is entitled to raise a defense, usually one of three basic defenses. First, the defendant may argue that the prosecution has not met its burden of proving each element of the alleged crime. For example, the defendant will claim that she did not commit the robbery. Thus, the elements of the crime of robbery have not been proven against her (although someone else may have committed the robbery). Second, the defendant may concede the she committed the elements of the crime of assault but that she did so for a greater social good, such as to defend herself from attack. Therefore, her response was "justified," and is thus not a crime. Third, the defendant may concede that she committed the elements of the crime. However, she will claim that, although no social good came of her actions, she should be "excused" from criminal liability because of special circumstances surrounding her actions, such as insanity. Defenses based on excuse will be the subject of the next chapter. Defenses based on justification are the subject of this chapter.

Self Defense and Defense of Others

In permitting defendants to raise the defense of justification through the Penal Law (Article 35), the legislature has in effect concluded that some actions, which would otherwise be criminal, are morally "superior" to the actions to which they responded. For example, self-defense and defense of others are the most prominent justification defenses. Normally, if someone intentionally killed or injured another person, she would be guilty of murder or assault. However, a person can use force against an attacker when she reasonably believes that the attacker is about to "use imminent unlawful physical force" (Penal Law 35.15(1)) against her or another person. However, before using deadly force, she must often retreat from the attacker if she can do so safely (Penal Law 35.15(2)(a)-(c)).

Assume that a police officer reasonably believes that a kidnapper is about to kill a child/victim. If the officer kills the kidnapper immediately, the officer will have killed one person (the kidnapper) to save one other person (the child/victim). However, the officer can never be sure that the kidnapper would have even killed the victim. But, under these circumstances, by justifying the officer's use of deadly force against the kidnapper, the legislature has said that it is morally (and perhaps economically) better to kill the kidnapper than to allow him the opportunity to kill the victim.

Self defense and defense of others can involve defensive force that is less than deadly force. For example, parents and teachers can use physical force to "maintain discipline or to promote the welfare of [children]" (Penal Law 35.10(1)). Wardens and operators of common carriers (Penal Law 35.10(2-3)) may use force to ensure order in the places over which they have responsibility, and police officers may use force to make an arrest or prevent an escape (Penal Law 35.30(1)). Normally, only reasonable force, not deadly force, can be used to protect property (Penal Law 35.25). An exception to this rule might arise in situations where an intruder was committing a burglary inside a dwelling.

Deadly force may be used to repel the imminent use of deadly force by an attacker (Penal Law 35.15(1) & (2)(a). But, in addition, the legislature permits deadly force to be used against an attacker to repel attacks on the person that fall short of threats of deadly force. Thus, deadly force may be used to stop a kidnapping, forcible rape, forcible sodomy, or robbery (Penal Law 35.15(2)(b), even where a perpetrator is not threatening deadly force. The legislature has decided that it is better to kill a potential kidnapper, sexual offender, or robber than to allow him to commit his intended felony, such as robbery.

Also, someone (such as an owner) in control of an occupied building or home (Penal Law 140.00(1-3) may use deadly force to terminate an arson or a burglary (Penal Law 35.20(2) & (3). Thus, in New York, the general rule is that reasonable force, or the least amount of force necessary, can be used to protect persons and property. Deadly force may be used only to prevent wrongdoers from committing intentional killings, kidnappings, forcible rapes and sodomies, arsons, robberies, and burglaries.

The main question involved in a defendant's claim of self-defense is determining whether the defendant's actions were "reasonable." If the defendant's actions were reasonable, then the defendant's killing of a deceased, for example, was justifiable. The defendant should be found not guilty of intentional murder. In contrast, if the defendant's killing of the deceased was unreasonable, then the defendant should be found guilty of an intentional murder (Penal Law 125.25(2)) and sentenced to a minimum of 15 years and a maximum of life in prison (Penal Law 70.00(2) (a) &(3)(a)(i).

Thus, it is crucial to determine how to examine what is "reasonable." What is reasonable to one person may be unreasonable to another. The particular cost of a salad in a fancy restaurant in a large city may be reasonable to a city dweller who lives in a high cost area. In contrast, the cost of the salad may be unreasonable to someone who lives in a rural farming area where vegetables for salads are grown on farms a mile away from the restaurant.

Similarly, a bully will view the need for self-defense differently from the pacifist. Thus, in New York, in determining whether the defendant who has asserted a self-defense claim acted reasonably, a jury will decide what a reasonable person in the defendant's situation would have perceived (an objective test). The jury will not consider what was actually in the mind of the bully, because a bully may view violence, subjectively, as always being necessary (a subjective test) (See Penal Law 35.15(2) and People v. Goetz, 68 N.Y.2d 96 (1986)).

In People v. Minaya, below, the court indicates how specific Penal Law provisions apply to claims of self-defense. Note that self-defense is a defense created, defined, and limited by the legislature. Examine when a defendant may raise a claim of self-defense. Note that a defendant must base a claim of self-defense on evidence that was introduced at trial. The evidence must meet a legal threshold before the judge, through jury instructions, may allow the jury even to consider claims of self-defense.

People v. Minaya (Ind. No. 01-01433) (Second Department) (2002-08674) (2004)

Opinion: Decision and Order. Appeal by the defendant from a judgment of the Supreme Court, Westchester County, rendered September 4, 2002, convicting him of assault in the first degree, criminal possession of a weapon in the third degree, reckless endangerment in the first degree, and reckless driving, upon a jury verdict, and imposing sentence. ORDERED that the judgment is reversed, on the law, and a new trial is ordered.

The defendant's conviction stemmed from an altercation on a New Rochelle street in the early morning hours of October 13, 2001. Pared to its essentials, the complainant, Luis Ceja, and a group of friends became embroiled in a melee with another group, including the defendant. Participants from both sides had been drinking, and some were armed with weapons such as belts, bats, and chains. According to his statement to police, when the defendant saw his friends being attacked, he entered his uncle's Volkswagen Jetta and drove toward his friends in an effort to provide them a means of escape. However, as he did so, one or more combatants jumped atop the Jetta, and began striking it; photographic evidence adduced at trial showed the hood and front windshield to have been badly dented and crushed, and the rear window was completely shattered and broken out. The defendant accelerated toward a wall and then applied the brakes, bringing the Jetta to a sudden stop; the photographs clearly show that the front of the Jetta was intact, it did not hit the wall. The complainant, however, was thrown from the car and he sustained serious physical injuries. The largely circumstantial evidence adduced by the prosecution sought to establish that the defendant struck the complainant deliberately, or acted with depraved indifference to the complainant's life.

The defendant was thus charged, inter alia, with first degree assault based on an intentional assault (Penal Law § 120.10[1]) and depraved indifference [*3] (Penal Law § 120.10[3]). At trial, the defendant asked for a justification charge, contending that he was justified in the use of the car to protect himself and/or his friends from the use of deadly physical force against them. The Supreme Court denied the request to charge. The defendant was acquitted of intentional assault, but was convicted of depraved indifference assault and lesser charges.

Viewing the evidence in the light most favorable to the prosecution, we find that it was legally sufficient to establish the defendant's guilt beyond a reasonable doubt. Moreover, upon the exercise of our factual review power, we are satisfied that the verdict of guilt was not against the weight of the evidence (see CPL 470.15[5]). Nevertheless, the judgment must be reversed and a new trial ordered.

Pursuant to Penal Law § 35.10(1), a person may use physical force to the extent he or she reasonably believes to be necessary to defend himself or herself or a third person from what he or she reasonably believes to be the use or imminent use of unlawful physical force. It is well settled that a justification charge should be given when there is any reasonable view of the evidence to support it (see People v Cox, 92 N.Y.2d 1002, 707 N.E.2d 428, 684 N.Y.S.2d 473). In this case, the Supreme Court denied the defendant's request for a justification charge concluding that the defendant could have driven away in complete safety without injuring the complainant. However, a reasonable view of the evidence supports the theory that the defendant initially sought to use the Jetta to rescue his outnumbered friends, and that he then was beset upon by one or more armed attackers who, while atop the Jetta, smashed the front windshield and completely destroyed the rear window. A reasonable view of the evidence thus supports the theory that the use of the Jetta was justified, that the defendant stopped short to escape the continued onslaught, and that the complainant was shed from the car as a result. Thus, the court erred in denying the defendant's request for a justification charge.

Examine the Cataldo case below to determine how to apply the rules surrounding self-defense. What kind of evidence must be produced before the judge should allow the jury even to consider self-defense? Consider the meaning of the concept of "initial aggressor." Does it matter who started a fight to determine whether someone can use force to defend himself? Can the person who started a fight claim self-defense?

People v. Cataldo, 260 A.D.2d 62, 688 N.Y.S.2d 265 (3rd Department 1999)

Defendant was indicted on one count of manslaughter in the first degree stemming from the fatal stabbing of Robert Hickey on July 18, 1997 in the Town of Owego, Tioga County. Defendant and Hickey were attending a party at a friend's home when an altercation arose during which Hickey confronted defendant for the purpose of provoking a fight. Hickey, however, was restrained by another friend from engaging in a physical confrontation.

Later, outside the residence, defendant was standing next to the driver's seat of his automobile with the door open, arguing with his girlfriend who was adjacent to the passenger-side door. Hickey again approached defendant and indicated that he wanted to fight. Defendant testified that as Hickey was standing in front of him, he squatted down and retrieved a knife from his car. Although none of the witnesses observed a knife displayed at any time, defendant asserted that he showed the knife to Hickey for the purpose of preventing the fight. According to witnesses who testified at trial, a fight ensued after Hickey pushed defendant who reacted by punching Hickey in [*663] the face. The altercation, which occurred primarily on the ground, ended when another individual was able to separate the two combatants. Thereafter, defendant left the scene in his automobile and Hickey was taken into the house. As a result of the fight, Hickey sustained a fatal stab wound to the abdomen and the left flank which pierced his spleen and kidney. He also suffered a deep cut on his left hand and a large cut on his forehead.

During the jury trial, defendant maintained that the wounds causing Hickey's death were accidentally inflicted and that he brandished the knife in order to dissuade Hickey from engaging in a fight. At the conclusion of trial, defendant was found not guilty of manslaughter in the first and second degrees, but found guilty of criminally negligent homicide. Defendant was sentenced to an indeterminate prison term of 1 to 4 years and now appeals.

Defendant contends that County Court erred in its refusal to charge justification (see Penal Law 35.05) for a second time in response to the jurors' request for instruction on the law of self-defense. In its initial charge to the jury, the court provided the instruction regarding justification pursuant to Penal Law 35.05 (2): "If you believe that the defendant displayed a knife as an emergency measure to avoid his imminent private injury which was about to occur by reason of a situation occasioned or developed through no fault of his own, then the defendant's conduct in displaying the knife, by itself, is not a criminal act." Thereafter, the charge relating to justification pursuant to Penal Law 35.15 was given which pertains to the "use of physical force in defense of a person." After the jury returned a verdict of guilty on the charge of criminally negligent homicide, County Court began to thank the jury for its efforts. A juror, however, inquired, "Isn't there one more part?", and the jury foreperson elaborated that it was "our understanding we were supposed to let you know when we had a verdict and then you would read to us about self-defense." After explaining to the jury that its procedural understanding was erroneous, the court asked whether the jury had reached a verdict and the foreperson responded that they had not. County Court then inquired whether the jurors remembered the instruction on self-defense or if they would like to have it read again. Since the foreperson indicated that the jury would like to have the charge read again, the court proceeded to reiterate the instruction pertaining to Penal Law 35.15 but denied defense counsel's request to charge justification pursuant to Penal Law 35.05 (2).

Penal Law 35.05 (2) grants discretion to the court to determine "whether the claimed facts and circumstances would, if established, constitute a defense." Having determined as a matter of law that, based on the evidence adduced at trial, a justification charge pursuant to Penal Law 35.05 (2) was appropriate (see Penal Law 35.05 [2]; and considering the jury's misapprehension regarding their deliberations, the charge needed to be included in supplemental instructions focusing on the defense of justification, which was of critical importance in this case. At trial the prosecutor argued that defendant was the initial aggressor of deadly physical force by virtue of his introduction of the knife into the fight, while in contrast the defense maintained that defendant was justified in wielding the knife to discourage the attack, thereby emphasizing the justification issue. Under the facts and circumstances of this case, and in light of the prejudice to defendant, the failure to provide both charges regarding justification in response to the jury's request operated to deprive defendant of a fair trial. Ordered that the judgment is reversed, on the law, and matter remitted to the County Court of Tioga County for a new trial.

Limitations on Self-Defense and Defense of Others

The Cataldo case illustrates that if the defendant claims self-defense and provides, through the evidence at trial, a sufficient basis for the claim, the judge presiding over the trial must instruct the jury about the law surrounding self-defense. However, although the defendant in Cataldo prevailed on his appeal and received a new trial, the law provides limitations on a self-defense claim. For example, the defendant claiming self-defense can prevail only if the defendant was not the "initial aggressor" (Penal Law 35.15(1)(a) & (b)). This means that the defendant cannot start a fight with a victim as a ruse to get the alleged victim to fight back so that the defendant can be "justified" in his beating of the victim in response.

Also, every person has a duty to retreat before resorting to deadly force (even if the force was otherwise justified), except unless a person is in her or his home (that is, a "dwelling") (Penal Law 35.15(2)(a). Even in a dwelling, the occupant may not use deadly force solely to oust an intruder. Deadly force can be used only to prevent the intruder from committing a crime in the dwelling (Penal Law 35.20(3)). In situations that do not involve a dwelling, a person who is contemplating self-defense must retreat from the defendant if he can do so safely. In essence, the legislature is saying that it is better for society to force people to run from rather than fight with bullies. There are logical exceptions to this rule. For example, law enforcement officers may use force to arrest a suspect or to prevent a suspect from escaping (Penal Law 35.30(1)).

The justification of self-defense can present many definitional problems. The following two cases discuss three of the important terms used in determining the extent and limits of self-defense: "initial aggressor," the "no duty to retreat" rule, and what constitutes a "dwelling." An additional issue addressed in the cases is the amount of force that can be used in self-defense.

People v. Carrera, 282 A.D.2d 614, 725 N.Y.S.2d 344 (2nd Department 2001)

During a struggle between the defendant and the deceased, the defendant stabbed the deceased in the chest with a steak knife. At trial, the defendant testified that the deceased swung what he believed to be an ice pick at his head. As they continued to struggle, the defendant stabbed the deceased. The "ice pick," which was actually a screwdriver, fell to the floor. The defendant then picked up the screwdriver and struck the deceased, causing contusions, abrasions, and puncture wounds. It was undisputed that the deceased was armed with the screwdriver before the encounter. None of the eyewitnesses, however, saw the screwdriver in the deceased's hand before he was stabbed. The Assistant Medical Examiner testified that the deceased died from the single knife wound to his chest. The trial court charged the jury on the defense of justification, but the jury found the defendant guilty of manslaughter in the second degree.

62

Viewing the evidence in the light most favorable to the prosecution ... we find that there was legally sufficient evidence from which the jury could have concluded, beyond a reasonable doubt, that the defendant was the initial aggressor. In reaching this conclusion, we have not considered the defendant's videotaped statement which was not admitted into evidence. Portions of that statement were admitted for the limited of impeachment. Contrary to the People's contention, the statement cannot be considered in assessing the sufficiency of the evidence.

The defendant correctly contends, however, that the trial court's charge on the use of excessive force was erroneous.... Even if a defendant is initially justified in using deadly physical force in self-defense, if he or she continues to use deadly physical force after the assailant no longer poses a threat, a jury may find that the defendant is no longer acting in self-defense....

The trial court's charge on excessive force misstated the applicable law and impermissibly permitted the jury to convict the defendant based upon a finding that he was not justified in inflicting the nonfatal wounds with the screwdriver subsequent to the stabbing. Moreover, even if the court had properly charged the jury on the use of excessive force, there was insufficient evidence from which the jury could have concluded that the defendant caused the deceased's death by the use of excessive force. The Assistant Medical Examiner testified that death was caused by the single stab wound to the chest, not by the alleged excessive force subsequently used. Since it cannot be determined whether the jury found that the defendant's conduct was not justified because he was the initial aggressor or because, although not the initial aggressor, he subsequently used excessive physical force, his conviction for manslaughter in the second degree must be reversed and a new trial ordered as to that crime.

Because we are ordering a new trial, we note an additional error with respect to the court's justification charge. The court charged the jury that the defendant was not justified in using deadly physical force if he knew he could retreat with complete safety.... However, there is no duty to retreat when the defendant is in his dwelling and is not the initial aggressor (see Penal Law 35.15 [2] [a] [i]). Because the evidence raised a factual question as to whether the area where the struggle occurred was part of the defendant's dwelling, that issue should have been submitted to the jury....

People v. Hernandez, 98 N.Y.2d 175, 774 N.E.2d 198, 746 N.Y.S.2d 434 (2002)

Defendant was convicted of manslaughter and criminal use of a firearm after he shot and killed James Carter inside the Bronx apartment building where defendant resided.... The morning of the shooting, Milagros Santiago and James Carter went to defendant's apartment and requested that repairs be undertaken in the Santiagos' apartment. Mary S. testified that she was present in the lobby and heard defendant respond by swearing and referring to Carter, who was African-American, in racially derogatory terms. Defendant and his brother (a building handyman) then accompanied Milagros and Mary S. upstairs to survey the damage while Carter stepped outside the building. After defendant loudly berated her for bringing Carter to his apartment to lodge a complaint, Milagros departed to find Carter.

Defendant, his brother and Mary S. soon left the Santiago apartment and began walking downstairs, meeting Carter and Milagros on the landing midway between the first and second floors. Carter asked defendant whether he had a problem and defendant responded "no problem." Mary S. testified that defendant told his brother he had to get something and would be back, and then he descended the remaining stairs and entered his apartment. Moments later, she heard a door open and defendant's wife say: "No, don't do it. Don't do it." Defendant responded: "Let me go. Let me go. I'm going to kill this black ...." Defendant proceeded up the stairs carrying a sawed-off shotgun. Carter tried to run up the stairs but defendant's brother blocked his path. Defendant then shot Carter in the chest and Carter collapsed on the landing.

Three police officers who heard the gunshot ran into the lobby where they discovered defendant standing near the bottom of the stairs. After they repeatedly directed defendant to drop his weapon, the officers disarmed him......

Defendant's trial testimony relating the events of that morning generally corresponded with that of Mary S. and the Santiagos until the verbal exchange with Carter on the stairwell. According to defendant, after he told Carter there was "no problem," he went into his apartment. About 40 minutes later, someone began banging on his door with such force that he feared the lock would give way. He asserted that, two weeks earlier, someone had knocked his door down while he and his family were not at home. He had been told by another building employee that the damage was inflicted by drug dealers who frequented the building.

Defendant and the building manager, who testified on his behalf, claimed the building was plagued by illegal drug activity. They contended that the front door of the building was missing and that the lock on the security gate had to be replaced on a daily basis because drug dealers would break the lock and use vacant apartments for their transactions. Although defendant testified that he had never seen Carter sell drugs, he believed that Carter was involved in drug activities in the building.

When the banging stopped, defendant retrieved a sawed-off shotgun from his closet. He asserted that he had found the gun in the basement months before but did not know it was loaded and did not know how to fire it. Carrying the shotgun, he stepped into the lobby and walked toward the stairwell when Carter jumped him from behind. In the course of this altercation, Carter grabbed the stock of the gun and pulled him up several stairs. Defendant testified that the gun "went off," although he had not cocked it and his hand was nowhere near the trigger, and Carter was shot at point blank range. Defendant stated that he turned around in shock and saw the police enter the building. He contended that he complied with police orders and submitted to arrest....

The sole issue on appeal is whether Supreme Court erred in denying defendant's request for a "no duty to retreat" instruction.... The provision reflects the principle, first established under the common law and long recognized by statute, that deadly physical force may be justified--with no criminal liability--if the deadly force was used in self-defense or in defense of others.... [D]eadly physical force is not justified if the person knows he or she can avoid the use of force by retreating with complete safety. The statute contains only one exception: there is no duty to retreat if a person is "in his [or her] dwelling and not the initial aggressor...."

Pivotal to defendant's argument is his contention that the lobby and stairwell areas were part of his dwelling.... In our view the word "dwelling," as used in Penal Law 35.15 (2) (a) (i), refers to a person's residence, and any definition of the term must therefore account for a myriad of living arrangements, from rural farm properties to large apartment buildings. For purposes of section 35.15, the determination of whether a particular location is part of a defendant's dwelling depends on the extent to which defendant (and persons actually sharing living quarters with defendant) exercises exclusive possession and control over the area in question. The term encompasses a house, an apartment or a part of a structure where defendant lives and where others are ordinarily excluded--the antithesis of which is routine access to or use of an area by strangers.

Considering the evidence in this case in the light most favorable to defendant and crediting, as we must, his testimony that he was attacked in the lobby, we conclude defendant was not entitled to a "no duty to retreat" jury instruction. The lobby and stairwell areas were used multiple times each day by tenants of the six-story apartment building and their guests. These areas were not under defendant's exclusive possession and could not fairly be characterized as defendant's living quarters. Accordingly, the lobby and common stairwell were not part of defendant's dwelling and Supreme Court did not err in declining to give a section 35.15 (2) (a) (i) charge....

Whether a person is entitled to the benefit of the "no duty to retreat" rule should not turn on how well protected the area in question is at the time of the attack. Such an approach would require a person to assess the security status of an area before deciding whether to attempt a retreat or to stand ground and resist an aggressor. Inequities in application of the rule would undoubtedly arise due to the greater likelihood that residents in secure buildings with locked doors and security guards would be afforded the benefit of the "no duty to retreat" charge while persons living in buildings without such protections and who may have more reason to feel threatened in their buildings would be denied the benefit of the charge. Here, for example, it is undisputed that both defendant and Carter had a right to be in the lobby at the time of the incident. Because the altercation would not have been avoided had a locked door or gate prevented intruders from entering the building, defendant's duty to retreat in the face of attack should not and does not rest on the presence or absence of such security devices.

Accordingly, the order of the Appellate Division should be affirmed....

Justification: Necessity or a Choice of Evils

New York provides an additional justification defense, which is called simply "justification" (Penal Law 35.05(2)). This defense is commonly known as "necessity" or the "choice of evils" in many other jurisdictions. When defendants raise the defense of necessity, they are essentially claiming, as with self-defense, that they were morally justified in their actions. For example, assume the following circumstance.

Four people are riding in a car on a narrow mountain road. The car is in perfect condition, and the driver is driving properly in every respect. Suddenly, a meteor falls from the sky and creates a hole 2000 feet deep just in front of the car. The driver has no time to stop. The driver has three options. His first option is to drive the car into the hole created by the meteor, in which case all four people in the car will die. His second option is to drive the car off the road and into a ravine 2000 feet below, in which case all four people in the car will die. His third option is to swerve into the opposite lane, where there is no hole. Unfortunately, a small child has wandered into that lane. If the driver drives into that lane, he knows his action will result in the death of the child, an event that, if not for the emergency situation caused by the meteor, would be a homicide.

If the driver decided to drive over the child and cause the child's death, the Penal Law (35.05(2)) would provide the driver with a defense. The defense (that is, justification/necessity/choice of evils) contains the following elements. A defendant, such as the driver, must show that (1) his conduct was required immediately; (2) the conduct was necessitated by an emergency; (3) the driver was not at fault in creating the emergency; and (4) the result of the conduct, such as the death of the child, was a lesser evil than the alternative, such as an automobile crash that would have resulted in four deaths.

Consider whether the law would ever sanction, in an emergency situation, the killing of one person to save only one other person. In the illustration above, what if the driver had been the only person in the car. Would the driver be justified in driving over the child to save his life? What if while driving the driver figured out a cure for cancer? Would the driver be justified then in running over the child? In the famous case of Dudley & Stephens (from England), noted below, determine whether the defendants could use Penal Law 35.05(2) to escape criminal responsibility. In particular, consider whether the shipwrecked sailors faced an "emergency." That is, could Dudley and Stephens have waited before committing their gruesome action?

The Queen v. Dudley & Stephens, 14 Q.B.D. (Queen's Bench Division) 273 (1884)

[The jury in the case found the following facts.]

[T]hat on July 5, 1884, the prisoners, Thomas Dudley and Edward Stephens, with one Brooks [another seaman in the lifeboat], all able-bodied English seamen, and the deceased [Richard Parker] also an English boy, between seventeen and eighteen years of age, the crew of an English yacht, a registered English vessel, were cast away in a storm on the high seas 1600 miles from the Cape of Good Hope, and were compelled to put into an open boat belonging to the said yacht. That in this boat they had no supply of water and no supply of food, except two 1 lb. Tins of turnips and for three days they had nothing else to subsist upon. That on the fourth day they caught a small turtle, upon which they subsisted for a few days, and this was the only food they had up to the twentieth day when the act now in question was committed.

That on the twelfth day the remains of the turtle were entirely consumed, and for the next eight days they had nothing to eat. They had no fresh water, except such rain as they from time to time caught in their oilskin capes. That the boat was drifting on the ocean, and was probably more than 1000 miles away from land. That on the eighteenth day, when they had been seven days without food and five without water, the prisoners spoke to Brooks as to what should be done if no succor came, and suggested that some one should be sacrificed to save the rest, but Brooks dissented, and the boy, to whom they were understood to refer, was not consulted. That on the 24th of July, the day before the act now in question, the prisoner Dudley proposed to Stephens and Brooks that lots should be cast who should be put to death to save the rest, but Brooks refused to consent, and it was not put to the boy, and in fact there was no drawing of lots.

That on the day the prisoners spoke of their having families, and suggested it would be better to kill the boy that their lives should be saved, and Dudley proposed that if there was no vessel in sight by the morrow morning the boy should be killed. The next day, the 25th of July, no vessel appearing, Dudley told Brooks that he had better go and have a sleep, and made signs to Stephens and Brooks that the boy had better be killed. The prisoner Stephens agreed to the act, but Brooks dissented from it. That the boy was then lying at the bottom of the boat quite helpless, and extremely weakened by famine and by drinking sea water, and unable to make any resistance, nor did he assent to his being killed. The prisoner Dudley offered a prayer asking forgiveness for them all if either of them should be tempted to commit a rash act, and that their souls might be saved. That Dudley, with the assent of Stephens, went to the boy, and telling him that his time was come, put a knife into his throat and killed him then and there; that the three men fed upon the body and blood of the boy four days; that on the fourth day after the act had been committed the boat was picked up by a passing vessel, and the prisoners were rescued, still alive, but in the lowest state of prostration.

That they were carried to the port of Falmouth, and committed for trial at Exeter. That if the men had not fed upon the body of the boy they would probably not have survived to be so picked up and rescued, but would within the four days have died before them. That at the time of the act in question there was no sail in sight, nor any reasonable prospect of relief. That under these circumstances there appeared to the prisoners every probability that unless they then fed or very soon fed upon the boy or one of themselves they would die of starvation. That there was no appreciable chance of saving life except by killing some one for the others to eat. That assuming any necessity to kill anybody, there was no greater necessity for killing the boy than any of the other three men. But whether upon the whole matter by the jurors found the killing of Richard Parker by Dudley and Stephens be felony and murder the jurors are ignorant, and pray the advice of the Court thereupon, and if upon the whole matter the Court shall be of the opinion that the killing of Richard Parker be felony and murder as alleged in the indictment.

[Dudley and Stephens were convicted of murder and sentenced to death. However, the Crown commuted their sentences to six months imprisonment.]

67

MULTIPLE CHOICE QUESTIONS

1. What is the test for determining what is the reasonable exercise of force in a self-defense case?
   A. What the defendant actually believed, a subjective test.
   B. What a reasonable person in the defendant's place would have done, an objective test.
   C. What a reasonable victim should have done, given all the facts and circumstances.
   D. None of the above.

2. Deadly force can be used to prevent:
   A. All felonies.
   B. All misdemeanors.
   C. Robbery.
   D. All the above.

3. A defendant cannot prevail on a claim of self-defense if he:
   A. Failed to retreat when he could have done so safely.
   B. Was the initial aggressor.
   C. Used deadly force to prevent the theft of a valuable car.
   D. None of the above.

4. In asserting a successful necessity defense, the defendant:
   A. Cannot have caused the death of any person.
   B. Cannot have acted to save a family member.
   C. Cannot have acted in emergency circumstances.
   D. None of the above.

5. The judge must give the jury an instruction on self-defense when:
   A. The prosecution denies the existence of self-defense.
   B. The defendant alleges the existence of self-defense.
   C. The evidence shows that a reasonable juror could conclude that the defendant acted in self-defense.
   D. All the above.

6. The court in the Hernandez case found that
   A. The extent of exclusive possession and control over a place can determine if that place is a "dwelling."
   B. Whether a person must retreat depends on the security of the area.
   C. The lobby of an apartment building is a "dwelling place."
   D. None of above.

DISCUSSION EXERCISES

1. Would the decision of the court in the Dudley and Stephens case have been different if the occupants of the lifeboat had drawn lots that included the victim?

2. Would there ever be a circumstance that would justify killing someone to save property? What if fire fighters in a fire truck needed to immediately run over a very ill elderly person blocking the road, who would die from disease in five minutes regardless, to arrive in time at a museum to save priceless, irreplaceable art from a raging fire?

3. Change the example in exercise 2 above so that the fire fighters need to arrive in time to save a building that contains the only formula for a drug that would cure cancer or prevent AIDS? Is not the formula merely property?

4. What policy considerations would influence the legislature to allow someone in her home to kill a burglar but not allow her to kill a car thief?

5. In allowing defenses based on justification, is the legislature really making a moral decision about certain events? Consider whether the legislature is simply making an economic cost-benefit analysis.

Chapter Seven

Defenses to Criminal Liability: Excuses

Introduction

Defendants raise defenses to criminal charges to try to eliminate or mitigate their legal responsibility. In asserting defenses based on justification, as discussed in the previous chapter, defendants are essentially arguing that society has sanctioned their action. Therefore, they should not be guilty of any crime, such as when they raise a successful self-defense claim. In contrast, when defendants raise a defense based on "excuse," they are in essence conceding that they committed some societal wrong. Defendants argue, however, that they should suffer limited or even no criminal liability because of the extraordinary circumstances surrounding their actions. The most prominent excuse defenses are insanity, duress, entrapment, and intoxication, which are discussed below.

Insanity

The major public policy behind permitting a defense based on insanity is that a defendant should not be liable for a crime that he or she did not understand was wrong. The theory is that if the defendant did not understand that what he was doing was wrong, then punishing him serves few public purposes. Punishment of an insane person would not deter future offenders, because someone who does not understand what he is doing will not be deterred from doing what he did by the punishment of a person in a prior case.

In New York, "insanity" is a defense based on "mental disease or defect" (Penal Law 40.15). To assert a successful mental disease or defect defense, a defendant must be able to prove that (1) because of mental disease or defect, (2) he lacked substantial capacity to (3) know or appreciate (4) the nature and consequences of his conduct or that his conduct was wrong.

Insanity defenses can involve gruesome fact situations because people who are insane sometimes commit deviant actions that they perceive at some level to be acceptable. For example, assume that a parent has a six-month-old child and is preparing a salad for dinner. The parent is using a large meat cleaver to cut the lettuce, cabbage, carrots, and celery. Because of a mental illness, however—a "mental defect" under the statute—the parent believes that the child's head is a head of cabbage and cuts the child's head. In a prosecution for assault—or murder, if the child dies—the parent should be found "not responsible by reason of mental disease or defect" (Criminal Procedure Law 330.10), because the parent lacked the "substantial capacity to know or appreciate the nature and consequences of her or his conduct" (Penal Law 40.15).

Similarly, assume that the same parent is watching television while preparing dinner. The parent believes, through the voice of the newscaster, that the devil, the only lawgiver in the world, is speaking to the parent. The devil tells the parent to assault or kill the child, which the parent does. Under this circumstance, the parent should also be found not responsible by reason of mental disease or defect, because the parent lacked the substantial capacity to know or appreciate that her or his conduct was wrong.

A successful defense based on mental disease or defect results in no criminal liability for the defendant. After such a defendant is found to be "not responsible by reason of mental disease or defect," the defendant will be examined (Criminal Procedure Law 330.20(2)) to determine whether he or she has a "dangerous mental disorder" or is "mentally ill or retarded" (Criminal Procedure Law 330.20(2)). If the defendant has no disorder and is not mentally ill, the defendant will usually be released from confinement and suffer no criminal or civil disabilities (Criminal Procedure Law 330.20(7)). If the defendant has a mental disorder or is mentally ill, the defendant will usually be confined in a mental institution under provisions in the Criminal Procedure Law or the Mental Hygiene Law (Criminal Procedure Law 330.20(7-22)).

Assume that a defendant concedes he has committed all the elements of the crime charged. In asserting an insanity defense, the defendant is saying, "At the time of the crime I was suffering from a mental disease or defect and I did not substantially appreciate that my actions were wrong or appreciate the nature of my actions." New York courts have struggled over the issue of whether it is fair to require such a defendant to prove his insanity, rather than requiring the prosecution to disprove his insanity. If a defendant was, and still might be, "insane," it might seem odd to make him bear the burden of proving insanity. He can assert insanity through the testimony of psychiatrists, but, because of the nature of his mental disease or defect, he may not be able to testify usefully on his behalf. The Kohl case below examines whether it is fair to place the legal burden on a defendant to prove his insanity. Examine the Kohl case to understand how the mental disease or defect defense operates in New York.

People v. Kohl, 72 N.Y.2d 191, 527 N.E.2d 1182, 532 N.Y.S.2d 45 (1988)

The decisive issue is whether Penal Law 40.15, defining New York's affirmative defense of mental disease or defect, violates the State constitutional Due Process Clause because Penal Law 25.00 (2) places the burden of proof by a preponderance of evidence on defendants for all affirmative defenses. We conclude that there is no State constitutional violation because placing this burden on the defendant does not relieve or transform the People's primary and constant burden of proving, beyond a reasonable doubt, all the elements of the crimes charged, including all components of the applicable culpable mental state element. Thus, we affirm the Appellate Division order upholding the conviction.

Defendant rented a house on a dairy farm in which he resided with his girlfriend and their infant son. On May 13, 1985, Peter Schiltz took his two sons, aged 2 and 3, with him to the dairy farm to deliver feed. When the delivery was completed, Schiltz lifted his sons into the front seat of his truck and started to leave. Defendant came out of his house and fired shots from a .12 gauge shotgun into the front seat. The initial shots killed one son and wounded the other and Schiltz. Returning to his house, defendant told his girlfriend that the man outside had sexually assaulted defendant's children. Defendant reloaded the gun and ran out screaming, "I got to get him. He's getting away." Schiltz had staggered to the barn where defendant stalked him, firing two more shots. Schiltz was on his hands and knees pleading for his life when defendant fired two final, fatal shots, saying, "Take that, you son of a bitch." The owner of the farm appeared and yelled, "Why, why did you do this?" Defendant said that Schiltz was going to pay one of his sons to sexually assault defendant's infant son. Before the police arrived, defendant assured his girlfriend, "They can't hurt me. I'm from another planet."

Defendant was charged with two counts each of intentional and depraved mind murder, second degree, and one count each of intentional and depraved mind assault, first degree. He waived his right to jury trial (CPL 320.10), and indicated that he would assert the affirmative defense of mental disease or defect (Penal Law 40.15).

At the bench trial, the prosecution at first concentrated on the factual developments by testimony of the eyewitnesses. The defense then called the defendant's girlfriend and his mother, who testified defendant frequently complained of severe head pains and exhibited bizarre behavior. Two psychiatrists, as experts for defendant, added that he was suffering from schizophrenia, paranoid type. The People presented two psychiatrists who, after examination of defendant, concluded he was not suffering from any mental disease or defect. Three of these psychiatrists agreed that at the time defendant fired the gun he intended to shoot his victims and that it was reasonable to conclude that defendant knew that firing a gun could kill his victims.

The trial court found defendant guilty of intentional murder of Schiltz, depraved mind murder of one son, and depraved mind assault of the other son. The trial court expressly found that "each and every element of those three counts * * * have been proven beyond a reasonable doubt" and that "defendant has failed to prove by a preponderance of the evidence that he should be found not guilty because he lacked criminal responsibility by reason of mental disease or defect."

In New York, criminal responsibility may be avoided if "as a result of mental disease or defect, [defendant] lacked substantial capacity to know or appreciate either: 1. The nature and consequences of such conduct; or 2. That such conduct was wrong" (Penal Law 40.15). Prior to 1984, the so-called insanity defense was catalogued as a traditional defense which the prosecution bore the burden of disproving beyond a reasonable doubt, in addition to its usual burden as to all elements of the crimes charged. The prosecution, of course, enjoyed the presumption that all persons are sane. Thus defendant, even under former law, bore some burden of coming forward with evidence rebutting the presumption of sanity. The presumption, however, was rebuttable: "[the] slightest creditable attack * * * even 'non-psychiatric proof' alone might overcome the presumption and sustain a verdict of acquittal." In 1984, after years of intensive study and debate, the Legislature repealed Penal Law 30.05 and substituted Penal Law 40.15, which made mental disease or defect an "affirmative" defense.

We thus hold that defendant was afforded State due process because New York's new scheme fits appropriately within sound precedents developed in cases analyzing pertinent statutory schemes under the Federal Constitution, which are also consistent with our own State's fundamental jurisprudence, values and history in the criminal law. Our substantive analysis begins with the axiom that in a criminal prosecution due process imposes on the prosecution the unalterable burden of proving beyond a reasonable doubt every element of the crime charged (In re Winship, 397 U.S. 358, 364). Defendant argues that the 1984 amendment violates the State constitutional due process guarantee in that it, in effect, transfers to defendant the legal responsibility of establishing innocence by disproving the culpable mental state—an essential element of the crime charged. The new statute does not do that.

Both the crime-defining statute and the affirmative defense one include consideration of and the production of evidence bearing on the defendant's mental state and processes at the time of the crime. However, the core of the People's proof and burden on the issue of criminal culpability established that defendant, at the time he fired the shots with respect to separate victims, "intended" his act, i.e., had a "conscious objective * * * to cause [the] result or to engage in [the] conduct" (Penal Law 15.05 [1]), and acted "recklessly," i.e., with "[awareness of] and [conscious] [disregard] [of] a substantial and unjustifiable risk that [the] result will occur or that [the] [circumstances] exist" (Penal Law 15.05 [3]). This was established by eyewitness testimony of defendant's actions and by his statements during and shortly after the shooting. Defendant, in turn, tried to establish by way of lay and expert testimony that he was "insane," a precise legal concept not necessarily inconsistent with the culpable mental state of legal intent or recklessness.

We must caution, however, that if one is unable to appreciate the nature and consequences of the conduct (Penal Law 40.15), it may be difficult to support a finding, at least in some cases, that the person had "conscious objective" to kill the victim (Penal Law 15.05 [1]; 125.25 [1]). For this reason, in a case where the concepts defined in those sections factually overlap with one another, it may be legally impossible in a given case for such a person to form a "conscious objective" to commit the crime. Then, the affirmative defense statute suffers the potential of impermissibly shifting to defendant the burden of disproving the formation of conscious objective to kill another human being, and the statute as applied could be unconstitutional. Thus, in a particular case, this potentiality could sow confusion and erroneous application of rules among juries with respect to the People's burden of proving the element of intent and defendant's burden of proving the affirmative defense of insanity.

This can be reasonably safeguarded by jury instructions which should emphasize the People's primary, ultimate, and nontransferable burden of proving all the elements of criminal intent beyond a reasonable doubt. Indeed, without transferring any burden to the defendant, the trial court should also, after the primary instructions, sequentially advise the jury that defendant bears a different burden on insanity, and that evidence of insanity relating to whether defendant knew what he was doing must be considered by the jury in its consideration of the People's nontransferable satisfaction of its burden to prove intent beyond a reasonable doubt. In this bench trial, of course, the Trial Judge served as finder of fact, and the defendant does not argue that the court improperly intermixed the respective burdens of proof.

Finally, the term mental disease or defect may have diverse meanings in the field of mental health, but it is for the Legislature, not the courts, to define what constitutes legal insanity in a criminal law context and to ascribe, within constitutional limits, the proper burden of proof for this exculpatory principle. Similarly, it is for the Legislature to define what constitutes a crime in this State, not the judiciary. Under Penal Law 125.25 (1), the burden on the prosecution is to prove that defendant intended to kill another human being and did kill that person or a third person. The modern statutory definition contains no explicit remnant of the common-law malice aforethought, or evil mind, and the prosecution burden is satisfied in this respect by proving that the defendant was capable of forming the conscious objective of committing the crime.

Accordingly, the order of the Appellate Division should be affirmed.

Duress

A duress defense is relatively rare. However, defendants may raise duress as a defense to argue that they were coerced into committing the crime with which they are charged by the "use or threatened imminent use of unlawful physical force upon the defendant or a third person" (Penal Law 40.00(1)). The defendant who asserts a defense of duress must be able to show that a person of reasonable firmness would not have been able to resist and that the defendant did not intentionally or recklessly place himself in a situation in which it is probable that he would be subjected to duress (Penal Law 40.00(2)). For example, if a drug kingpin kidnaps an innocent stranger and threatens to kill the stranger if the stranger does not rob a bank, the stranger could probably assert a successful duress defense (meaning the elimination of criminal liability through a verdict of "not guilty") if he robbed the bank and were prosecuted for robbery. In contrast, if the drug kingpin ordered one of his drug dealers to commit the robbery under the same circumstances, the worker could probably not assert a successful duress defense, because the worker placed herself in a situation where workers were commonly ordered to commit robberies.

The Crumpler case, noted below, illustrates the defense of duress in New York. Consider what level of force or threat must be present before a duress defense will be appropriate.

People v. Crumpler, 242 A.D.2d 956, 662 N.Y.S.2d 341 (4th Department 1997)

On this appeal from a judgment convicting him of robbery in the first degree (Penal Law 20.00, 160.15 [4]), defendant argues that Supreme Court erred in charging, over his objection, the affirmative defense of duress. Defendant argues in the alternative that the court's decision to charge the affirmative defense, made only after defense counsel had delivered his summation in reliance upon the court's earlier ruling that it would not charge duress, deprived him of a fair trial. We conclude that a fair reading of the record establishes that the affirmative defense of duress was raised and that the jury should have been charged with that defense. We conclude, however, that defendant was unduly predjudiced when the court charged the defense after defense counsel had delivered his summation in reliance upon the court's determination not to charge duress, requiring reversal.

On April 26, 1995, at about 4:45 A.M., a McDonalds Restaurant at 1420 Lyell Avenue in Rochester was robbed by three men, one of whom brandished a gun. The men forced the assistant manager, at gunpoint, to open the safe. Defendant, the only other employee in the store at the time, initially indicated to the police that he was in the grill area at the time of the robbery and did not see anything. He eventually admitted that he had been approached by three men as he walked to work that morning, one of whom had a gun. The man held the gun to his head and demanded that defendant turn off the alarm and leave the door unlocked when he arrived at work. The man also told defendant that he knew where defendant lived and threatened to "shoot up" defendant's house if defendant did not comply with his demands. Defendant testified that he complied with the demands because he feared for his safety and that of his coworker and family.

The People requested that the court charge the affirmative defense of duress, but defendant objected, arguing that he had not raised the duress defense. The court declined to charge duress, but stated that it would charge the jury that there exists in the law a duress defense, that it would define the duress defense for the jury, and that it would indicate to the jury that the duress defense was not being raised in this case. Defense counsel objected, and, when the court insisted on that course of action, defense counsel requested that the court charge the affirmative defense of duress. The prosecutor joined in the request to charge the affirmative defense, but the court refused to do so. Defense counsel delivered his summation in reliance upon the assurance of the court that it would not charge the affirmative defense of duress. During summation, counsel emphasized defendant's lack of intent and argued that defendant's conduct was motivated by fear.

Following summations, the court determined that it would charge the affirmative defense of duress. Defense counsel requested a mistrial, arguing that it would be prejudicial for the court to give that charge after defense counsel had delivered his summation in reliance upon the court's assurance that the charge would not be given. The court denied the motion and charged the jury on the affirmative defense of duress.

We agree with the People that the record establishes that the affirmative defense of duress was raised and should have been charged. We agree with defendant, however, that the court erred in charging the affirmative defense of duress after defense counsel had delivered his summation in reliance upon the court's ruling that the defense would not be charged. The untimely reversal by the court of its prior ruling resulted in prejudice to defendant and requires reversal.

Entrapment

Like duress, entrapment is a relatively rare defense. To assert a successful entrapment defense, a defendant must be able to show that he or she was induced to commit a crime by a public servant, such as a law enforcement officer, and that the methods used created a substantial risk that the offense would be committed by a person who was otherwise not disposed to commit it (Penal Law 40.05). The key for the defendant is to show that he or she was not predisposed to commit the charged offense. The lack of predisposition can be very difficult for the defendant to prove, because the vast majority of people will commit none of the crimes that are usually the subject of an entrapment defense, even if they are afforded the opportunity to do so. The Brown case below illustrates the use of the entrapment defense in a prostitution case.

People v. Brown, 82 N.Y.2d 869, 631 N.E.2d 106, 609 N.Y.S.2d 164 (1993)

Defendant was convicted in Syracuse City Court of patronizing a prostitute in the fourth degree (Penal Law 230.03). County Court, Onondaga County, affirmed the conviction. Defendant's principal argument on appeal to this Court is that it was reversible error for the Trial Judge to deny his request for a jury charge on the affirmative defense of entrapment (Penal Law 40.05). We affirm, finding no evidentiary basis on this record to warrant the requested instruction.

A trial court must charge entrapment on a defendant's request where the evidence adduced at trial, when viewed in the light most favorable to the defendant, reasonably and sufficiently supports the defense. Defendant bore the burden of establishing entrapment by a preponderance of the evidence (Penal Law 25.00 [2]), that is, to demonstrate that: (1) he was actively induced or encouraged to commit the offense by a public official; and (2) such inducement or encouragement created a "substantial risk" that the offense would be committed by defendant who was not otherwise disposed to commit it (Penal Law 40.05.

There was trial testimony adduced by the People that at approximately 10:45 p.m. on May 22, 1991 a male undercover police sergeant dressed as a female was standing near a street corner in the City of Syracuse when defendant pulled over to the adjacent curb in front of him. The undercover officer testified that he approached the front passenger window of the car and asked defendant if he was looking for a date; defendant said he was; the officer asked defendant how much he was spending; defendant said "20 or 25"; the officer asked defendant if he wanted oral sodomy for 25, and defendant said yes. He directed defendant to drive around the corner, which defendant did, and back-up police units arrested him. An undercover police lieutenant positioned in a nearby unmarked surveillance vehicle overheard the conversation and corroborated its contents. The undercover officers and the defendant agreed that the conversation lasted approximately 15 to 30 seconds.

By contrast, defendant testified that while driving to pick up food he stopped at a stop sign at the intersection in question, where a man dressed as a woman approached his vehicle, asked him what he was looking for, and offered to perform oral sodomy for money. Defendant testified he did not respond to the offer. He denied ever agreeing to exchange money for sex or voluntarily pulling over when he turned the corner.

Under no reasonable view of this evidence could a jury have found that the statutory requirements of an entrapment affirmative defense were satisfied. Defendant's testimony denying that he committed the proscribed conduct does not alone support or defeat the requested charge. The testimony of the undercover officers demonstrates that they merely afforded defendant an opportunity to commit the offense, which standing alone is insufficient to warrant an entrapment charge. Merely asking a defendant to commit a crime is not such inducement or encouragement as to constitute entrapment. Defendant's remaining contentions are without merit. Order affirmed, in a memorandum.

Intoxication

In New York, intoxication can be used as a defense to "negative an element of the crime charged" (Penal Law 15.25). This means that a defendant can, in essence, argue that he or she was unable to form the mental state required of a certain crime because of intoxication. A person's "intoxication" can result from alcohol, illegal drugs, and even legal drugs and substances.

To illustrate, assume that a defendant claims he was intoxicated when he shot and killed a victim. The defendant argues that he could not form the intent necessary to be guilty of an intentional murder (Penal Law 125.25(1)). The defendant may argue that the shooting was a reckless or negligent act engaged in while drunk, in which case the defendant would still be guilty of manslaughter in the second degree (Penal Law 125.15(1)) or criminally negligent homicide (Penal Law 125.10) respectively.

In the Westergard case below, the defendant raises the defense of intoxication, and the New York Court of Appeals discusses what evidence is sufficient to raise intoxication as a defense to a crime that has "intent" as its required mental state.

People v. Westergard, 69 N.Y.2d 642, 503 N.E.2d 1018, 511 N.Y.S.2d 587 (1986)

The order of the Appellate Division should be affirmed.

Defendant, charged with burglaries of several Poughkeepsie businesses in the early morning of January 24, 1983, at trial contended that his chronic alcoholism and drug abuse constituted a disease or serious mental disorder short of insanity that relieved him of liability for those crimes. This defense was supported by his own testimony, as well as that of his brother and a psychologist. Defendant testified that in January 1983 he was an active alcoholic. On the evening in question, he had gone from bar to bar drinking and eating dried mushrooms, then he entered a store and took money from the cash register, kicked a hole in a wall and stole change from the cash register in an adjoining store, and tore the coin box from a cigarette machine. His brother testified that defendant had been drinking the evening of the burglaries, that defendant (then 21) had been drinking heavily since he was 12 or 13 years old, that when he drank he became violent and uncontrollable, and that he also used drugs, often in combination with alcohol. A psychologist testified that alcoholism is a recognized disease. Having twice interviewed defendant in late 1983, he gave his opinion that defendant is an alcoholic, that he behaved typically for an alcoholic the night in question, that he was intoxicated, and that he was incapable of "acting purposefully with regard to a conscious objective" but acted out of rage. Three prosecution witnesses who had seen defendant in the critical hours of January 24, 1983 gave their opinion that defendant was not intoxicated.

Defendant's requested charges of diminished capacity and diminished capacity to form a specific mental state were both denied. His request for an intoxication charge was granted. The jury was instructed that, while intoxication is not a defense to a criminal charge, intent to commit a burglary—a conscious objective to engage in such conduct— must be established and that evidence of defendant's alleged intoxication could be considered in determining whether or not his mind was so obscured by the consumption of alcohol or drugs that he was incapable of forming the requisite intent. The jury returned a verdict of guilty of two counts of burglary in the third degree and one count of criminal trespass in the third degree, and the Appellate Division affirmed, one Justice dissenting. On appeal to this court, defendant challenges the refusal of his request to charge diminished capacity as bearing on the issue of intent, and also the trial court's limitation of his parents' testimony.

The trial court did not err in its refusal to charge diminished capacity as bearing on the issue of intent. While proof of a mental defect other than insanity may "in a particular case negate a specific intent necessary to establish guilt," the Legislature has made specific provision regarding proof of intoxication. Evidence of intoxication "may be offered by the defendant whenever it is relevant to negate an element of the crime charged." (Penal Law 15.25.) Such evidence was received here, including expert testimony that on January 24, 1983 defendant, acting as a functioning alcoholic, became intoxicated and was rendered "incapable of acting purposefully with regard to a conscious objective." On this record, the court adequately instructed the jury regarding the possible effect of defendant's condition on January 24, 1983 on his state of mind. No additional instruction was required.

Nor did the court abuse its discretion by limiting the testimony of defendant's parents to events of the night of the burglaries and excluding their testimony concerning past events.

MULTIPLE CHOICE QUESTIONS

1. Which of the following is an affirmative defense in New York?
   A. Insanity.
   B. Duress.
   C. Entrapment.
   D. All the above.

2. The theory behind defenses of insanity, duress, and entrapment is:
   A. Justification.
   B. Excusal.
   C. Affirmative defenses.
   D. All the above.

3. Fill in the blank. The prosecution will _____ request a jury instruction on duress.
   A. Never.
   B. Always.
   C. Sometimes.
   D. None of the above.

4. With regard to entrapment, the key issue will usually relate to:
   A. Whether the police informant or officer is credible.
   B. Whether the police focused on obtaining evidence against the defendant.
   C. Whether the defendant was predisposed to commit the crime.
   D. All the above.

5. From the defendant's perspective, the purpose of an intoxication defense is to:
   A. Show that the conduct at issue was not voluntary.
   B. Negate the mental state that is an element of the crime.
   C. Show the effects of alcoholism.
   D. All the above.

DISCUSSION EXERCISES

1. What do the penal law and the court cases mean when they indicate that defense are "affirmative defenses"?

2. What are the public policy reasons behind permitting defendants to raise "excuse" defenses?

3. Which party—prosecution or defense—does the current "mental disease or defect" test favor, and why?

4. Under New York's test for duress, would a defendant be entitled to raise a duress defense if she claimed that she intentionally killed a victim because she was being threatened with death from an evil person if she did not kill the victim?

5. Do you agree with the finding of the trial court in the insanity case above, People v. Kohl? Why or why not?

6. Why should the legislature even recognize an entrapment defense? What does it matter if a government agent did something that encouraged a defendant to commit a crime? If the defendant knew that his actions constituted a crime, why should he receive any benefit if he found the courage to commit the crime?

7. What if an intoxicated defendant, in addition to claiming that he could not have formed the intent to kill, also argues that "I was so drunk I didn't know what I was doing when I pulled my gun and shot and killed the victim?" If the defendant really was that drunk, should he be "not guilty" of any crime, including a reckless or negligent homicide?

8. Does intoxication ever prevent someone from doing something he or she did not intend to do? Could the prosecution argue that intoxication may make someone less inhibited, but it does not affect, for example, his intent to pull the trigger of a gun and kill someone? If someone was truly so intoxicated she could not form the intent to commit a crime, then would that person not be "insane?"

Chapter Eight

Crimes against Persons I: Criminal Homicide

Introduction

In New York, the term "homicide" refers to conduct that causes a death. Homicide includes the crimes of murder, manslaughter, criminally negligent homicide, abortion, and self-abortion (Penal Law 125.00). To prove a homicide, the prosecution must prove that with a (1) mental state of intent, depraved indifference, recklessness, or negligence the defendant (2) caused (3) the death of a (4) person or a miscarriage in a female when the female has been pregnant for more than 24 weeks.

Classifying Homicides

In New York and many other states, the classification of the various homicides can be extremely confusing, because the states attach many different names (such as murder and manslaughter) to certain crimes to indicate various levels of moral culpability. In reality, most of the distinction between the different types of homicides relates to mental states. For example, in New York, a defendant who intentionally kills another person under circumstances that would justify the death penalty (such as when the victim is a police officer or witness) will be guilty of murder in the first degree (Penal Law 125.27). A defendant who intentionally kills a person (absent special circumstances) will be guilty of murder in the second degree (Penal Law 125.25(1)). A defendant who recklessly kills another person will be guilty of manslaughter in the second degree (Penal Law 125.15). A defendant who negligently kills another person will be guilty of criminally negligent homicide (Penal Law 125.10).

Exceptions to the Requirement of a Mental State

Like the vast majority of other states, New York authorizes a homicide conviction (murder in the second degree under Penal Law 125.25(3)) under one circumstance in which the defendant has exhibited no culpable mental state with regard to a homicide, or perhaps at most only a mental state of negligence or recklessness. This circumstance is popularly known as "felony murder." The classic case involves a defendant who agrees to serve as a "getaway" driver for accomplices in a bank robbery. The defendant, who is the driver, may know that the accomplices have guns. All of the robbers , however, agree that they will not shoot their guns. They may even explicitly agree that they will not harm anyone. The defendant, the getaway driver, may even have explicitly told the accomplices never to use any type of force. If during the robbery, however, one of the accomplices gets frightened and fires a warning bullet into the air, and that bullet ricochets off the ceiling and causes the death of an innocent person, the defendant who is the "getaway" driver, as well as every other robber or accomplice, can be liable for murder in the second degree.

In reality, the defendant who is the getaway driver may have "only" recklessly helped cause the death of an innocent person. By participating in the robbery, however, the defendant/getaway driver is assumed by New York law to have understood the risk that the dangerous act of robbery would create for other people. Thus, the defendant would be guilty of murder in the second degree under New York law (Penal Law 125.25(3)).

States have a felony murder rule to deter certain felonies that are inherently dangerous to human life. These felonies are usually limited to robbery, burglary, kidnapping, arson, certain rapes and sodomies, and escape from prison. All defendants who are responsible for the underlying felony, regardless of their involvement in the killing, can be convicted of "felony murder" if an innocent person dies in the course of the felony.

The felony murder rule elevates to murder a reckless act that results in death. In contrast, an intentional killing that would otherwise be murder may sometimes be transformed into the less severe crime of "manslaughter in the first degree" (Penal Law 125.20(2)). A reduction from murder to manslaughter may happen where the defendant was acting in the "heat of passion," such as when the defendant kills his wife after finding her engaged in sexual intercourse with another man. Thus, in New York, the defendant can argue that he or she should be convicted of manslaughter in the first degree—instead of murder in the second degree—because the defendant acted "under the influence of extreme emotional disturbance" while intentionally killing some person (Penal Law 125.20(2)). Although many states limit this type of defense to cases where the defendant finds a spouse engaged in some type of sexual relations with another person, New York's statute allows defendants in any circumstance to argue that they intentionally killed someone while under "extreme emotional disturbance." A jury finding of extreme emotional disturbance results in a conviction for manslaughter in the first degree and a maximum sentence of 25 years, rather than a conviction for murder and a maximum sentence of life.

To analyze the extreme emotional disturbance defense, examine the Harris case, noted below. In most circumstances in life, the average person will not kill another person, even while enduring the most grievous circumstances, such as finding a spouse with another person. A very few people, however, when confronted with hurtful circumstances, will act violently against a spouse or other person who is perceived to have humiliated or harmed them. The extreme emotional disturbance defense allows these persons to receive favorable treatment under the law when they kill their spouses. The Harris case discusses this point.

People v. Harris, 95 N.Y.2d 316, 740 N.E.2d 227, 717 N.Y.S.2d 82 (2000)

Defendant was convicted after a jury trial of murder in the second degree (Penal Law 125.25[1]). The evidence established that defendant killed his long-time friend, Larry Amorose, with a machete. With the help of his girlfriend, defendant decapitated and dismembered Amorose's body, put the body parts in garbage bags and discarded the bags in the ocean off Coney Island.

The trial court rejected defendant's request for a charge on extreme emotional disturbance (Penal Law 125.25[1][a]) on the ground that the evidence was insufficient to justify submission of that affirmative defense to the jury. The Appellate Division affirmed the judgment of conviction and a Judge of this Court granted defendant leave to appeal. We now reverse.

The Legislature has recognized that some intentional homicides may result from "an understandable human response deserving of mercy." Thus, the fact "that [a] homicide was committed under the influence of extreme emotional disturbance constitutes a mitigating circumstance reducing murder to manslaughter in the first degree" (Penal Law 125.20[2]). Mitigation is not limited to circumstances associated with the traditional "heat of passion" doctrine, but may be considered with respect to a broad range of situations where the trier of fact believes that such leniency should be afforded an emotionally disturbed defendant.

Hence, Penal Law 125(1)(a) provides that it is an affirmative defense to the crime of murder in the second degree that "the defendant acted under the influence of extreme emotional disturbance for which there was a reasonable explanation or excuse, the reasonableness of which is to be determined from the viewpoint of a person in the defendant's situation under the circumstances as the defendant believed them to be." The determination whether a defendant is entitled to a charge on extreme emotional disturbance requires the trial court to assess whether sufficient evidence was presented "for the jury to find by a preponderance of the evidence that the elements of the affirmative defense are satisfied."

The extreme emotional disturbance defense requires proof of both subjective and objective elements. The subjective element focuses on the defendant's state of mind at the time of the crime and requires sufficient evidence that the defendant's conduct was actually influenced by an extreme emotional disturbance. This element is generally associated with a loss of self-control.

The objective element requires proof of a reasonable explanation or excuse for the emotional disturbance. Whether such a reasonable explanation or excuse exists must be determined by viewing the subjective mental condition of the defendant and the external circumstances as the defendant perceived them to be at the time, "however inaccurate that perception may have been, and assessing from that standpoint whether the explanation or excuse for [the] emotional disturbance was reasonable."

People v Moye (66 N.Y.2d 887, 498 N.Y.S.2d 767, 489 N.E.2d 736) provides an apt illustration of proof warranting the submission to the jury of the extreme emotional disturbance defense. The defendant in that case admitted, in statements to the police and District Attorney's Office, that he decapitated and eviscerated a woman who teased and ridiculed him for his inability to perform sexual intercourse with her. Addressing the subjective element of the extreme emotional disturbance defense, we held that the defendant's "savage acts of mutilating and decapitating his victim, coupled with his statements to the police and District Attorney that 'something snapped' inside him when

83

she mocked and taunted him, that he went 'bananas' and he needed help, were evidence of a loss of self-control associated with the defense." As for the objective element, we held that "there was sufficient evidence for submission to the jury—which a rational jury might have accepted or rejected—of an explanation or excuse for defendant's emotional state, in his recounting of the victim's continued ridicule and taunting about his impotence."

In our view, the present case is analytically indistinguishable from Moye. Thus, viewing the evidence in the light most favorable to the defendant, as we must in considering whether the extreme emotional disturbance defense should have been charged to the jury, we conclude that defendant presented sufficient evidence with respect to both elements of the defense of extreme emotional disturbance so as to be entitled to the charge. Defendant confessed to the murder. His handwritten and videotaped statements to the police and District Attorney's Office were introduced into evidence by the People. Defendant explained that he was in love with his live-in girlfriend, Monique Lloyd, and that Amorose started talking to her. Lloyd had been unfaithful to defendant with Amorose in the past. Indeed, she once left defendant for Amorose. When Lloyd went to another room, Amorose began taunting defendant by expressing in crude terms that he could still have sex with Lloyd at anytime and that Lloyd would leave defendant for him merely at his beck and call.

Like the statements in Moye, defendant's confessions explained that he completely lost control over his actions in response to Amorose's taunts. Defendant related that he started hitting Amorose and that "it was like [he] was looking at a movie [and] didn't have any control" at the time. He admitted that he just "couldn't stop" his attack on Amorose. He stated that he started crying and vomiting after he killed Amorose with the machete. He then related how he cut his victim to pieces. Additional evidence relevant to both elements of the defense was introduced in the form of psychiatric testimony. Based upon diagnostic analysis and review of pertinent records, defendant's psychiatric expert opined that defendant was acting under "extreme stress" at the time of the incident and that he satisfied the criteria equated with "the legal terminology" of extreme emotional disturbance. The expert also explained that defendant's comment—that he felt as if he were looking at a movie when he lost control over his actions—described a psychological phenomenon known as derealization, which often occurs "in extreme stress situations." The expert further testified that defendant suffered from post-traumatic stress disorder as a result of previous traumatic incidents involving extreme violence, including defendant's presence as an eyewitness to a murder. The expert relied upon this diagnosis, and other psychological factors that shaped how defendant perceived the world and events leading up to the slaying of Amorose, to explain why, in his opinion, a reasonable explanation existed for defendant's disturbed state of mind.

Relying upon other portions of defendant's statements and expert testimony, the People argue that defendant did not suffer from any extreme emotional disturbance but acted solely out of anger and jealousy and then in self-defense. However, this merely presented conflicts in the evidence that raised issues of fact for the jury to resolve in determining whether to accept or reject the affirmative defense of extreme emotional disturbance. Where, as here, the defendant's request for submission of the extreme emotional disturbance defense to the jury should have been granted, the trial court's failure to charge the defense requires a reversal and new trial. In light of our determination, we need not consider defendant's remaining arguments. Accordingly, the order of the Appellate Division should be reversed and a new trial ordered.

Homicide and Unborn Children

As mentioned above, New York law provides that homicide can also include the killing of an unborn child or fetus when the woman carrying the fetus has been pregnant for more than 24 weeks (Penal Law 125.00). This statute enforces the state's interest in protecting unborn children, as discussed in the famous U.S. Supreme Court case of Roe v. Wade, 410 U.S. 113 (1973).

Not all states consider the killing of an unborn child to be homicide; only twenty-nine have "fetal homicide" statutes. Among those states that do consider the killing of an unborn child to be homicide, most criminalize the killing of a fetus at all stages of pregnancy, if special circumstances exist. New York is among the group of states that only criminalize the killing of an unborn child in the later stages of pregnancy.

New York's fetal homicide statute, however, conflicts with a separate New York statutory provision providing that a "person" who is the victim of a homicide must be a "human being who has been born and is alive" (Penal Law 125.05). The following case illustrates how one lower New York court resolved the conflict between these two provisions.

People v. Joseph, 496 N.Y.S.2d 328, 130 Misc.2d 377 (County Court, 1985)

Defendant is charged with multiple counts of Criminally Negligent Homicide and Vehicular Manslaughter, among other charges, for conduct alleged to have caused the death of Donna Nehme, and the subsequent stillbirth of her child. Counts 9, 10, and 11 charge the defendant with these offenses due to the "death" of a victim identified in the indictment as "The Stillborn Nehme." The defendant moves for the dismissal of Counts 9, 10, and 11, asserting that the "death" of an unborn child cannot support a prosecution for the offenses charged.

The defendant argues that Penal Law Section 125.10, Criminally Negligent Homicide, and Penal Law Section 125.12, Vehicular Manslaughter, both require proof of the death of a person, and that Penal Law Section 125.05(1) defines a person as "a human being who has been born and is alive." It is axiomatic that for the People to prove the commission of a crime, they must be able to prove each and every element of the offense as set forth in the Penal Law. The People concede that the alleged victim of the offenses charged in Counts 9, 10, and 11, was not a "person" so defined. The People, however, point to Section 125.00, which section defines a homicide as: conduct which causes the death of a person or an unborn child with which a female has been pregnant for more than twenty-four weeks under circumstances constituting murder, manslaughter in the first degree, manslaughter in the second degree, criminally negligent homicide, abortion in the first degree, or self-abortion in the first degree.

The People contend that … this definition of homicide effectively includes "an unborn child with which a female has been pregnant for more than twenty-four weeks" within the purview of the specific offenses set forth in the Penal Law under the heading of homicide. The People cite no authority for this position, and the case appears to present a matter of first impression.

At common law, a person could not be convicted of homicide for the death of a child as a result of prenatal injuries unless the child was first born alive….The law of the State of New York requires that in every case other than illegal abortion, the victim of a homicide be a "person" and provides the statutory definition of person set forth above. This is the same definition which obtained at common law, and this court agrees …that only a clear legislative pronouncement will support a different interpretation. In seeking such a pronouncement, the People wrongly rely upon Section 125.00, which provides a definition of the entire class of offenses designated homicides, and which by virtue of the inclusion of abortion in the list of offenses must necessarily include an unborn child in the list of victims. A review of the legislative history of this section admits to no larger significance.

In 1965, the Penal Law of the State of New York was completely revised. The homicide law in effect at that time, which can be traced to an 1869 enactment, provided that "the willfull killing of an unborn quick child, by any injury committed upon the mother of such child, is manslaughter in the first degree," Former Section 1050(2). This law was itself a departure from the common law, although it availed itself of the common law term "quick." The question of just when a child was "quick" was almost immediately a source of litigation. However, in the century which followed this enactment before the 1965 revisions, this Court can find no case in which the statute was used to prosecute a homicide other than an illegal abortion. Indeed, in the 1949 case of People v. Hayner, 300 N.Y. 171, 90 N.E.2d 23, a homicide prosecution involving the gruesome killing of a child as it was being delivered, one finds the Court of Appeals insisting upon proof that the child had been "born" within the common law definition of "wholly expelled from its mother's body and possessed or was capable of an existence by means of a circulation independent of her own…."

While the 1965 revision attempted to clarify the codification of these common law principles, this Court can find no evidence the revision was intended to alter them. The 1965 revision consolidated several scattered references to abortion into more concise provisions entirely within the homicide article, and included abortion in an introductory definition of homicide similar to that upon which the People now rely. The section provided that the term "homicide" would include abortion in the first degree, and defined the class of victims of homicide as including "an unborn child with which a female has been pregnant for more than twenty-four (24) weeks." This definition was necessary because the same article provided the offense of abortion in the second degree, which prohibited abortions at an earlier point in the term, but which was not to be considered a homicide. Following Section

125.00 in both the 1965 enactment and in the law in its current form are the specific definitions for the various homicide offenses, and in every case other than abortion, the statutes required, as they do now, that the victim be a person within the common law appreciation of the term. The commentators note that the Section 125.05 definition of person was included to insure that the death of a "person" would not include abortional killing of an unborn child, People v. Ebasco Services, Inc., 77 Misc.2d 784, 354 N.Y.S.2d 807. It is equally clear to this Court that the Legislature did not intend to make the non-abortional killing of an unborn child a homicide…. It is certainly within the exclusive province of the Legislature to provide a criminal sanction for the non-abortional killing of an unborn child, and it is the opinion of this Court that the Legislature has not so provided. The Legislature had the opportunity to do so in its lengthy deliberations concerning the proposed Penal Law and the several reports of the drafting commission. However, neither the law enacted in 1965 nor the twenty years of subsequent legislative and judicial action demonstrate a desire to abrogate a five hundred year old principle of common law. The Court must dismiss Counts 9, 10, and 11 of the indictment, dealing with the stillbirth of the Nehme's child.

Aggravating Factors and the Death Penalty

As mentioned above in Chapter 2, New York law provides for the death penalty in certain homicide cases. Penal Law 125.01, enacted in 1995 after an earlier death penalty statute was struck down as unconstitutional in 1984, states that a defendant may be sentenced to death if the prosecution proves any one of thirteen aggravating factors. Since enactment of the new death penalty law, the New York Court of Appeals has struggled to interpret it; to date, no defendant's death penalty sentence has been upheld by the Court, although the Court has carefully avoided ruling on the constitutionality of the law. The following case illustrates how death penalty issues interplay with different levels of homicides.

People v. Cahill, --- N.E.2d ---, 2003 WL 22770167 (2003)

Under New York's capital punishment scheme, a person who commits an intentional (second degree) murder is eligible for a death sentence if any one of 13 aggravating factors is proved (see Penal Law 125.27[1][a][i]-[xiii]) ….In the case before us, a jury found defendant guilty of two counts of first degree murder, based on two aggravating factors (witness elimination murder, Penal Law 125.27[1][a][v], and intentional murder in the course of and in furtherance of second degree burglary, Penal Law 125.27[1][a][vii]). At the penalty phase of the trial, the jury determined that defendant should be sentenced to death on both counts. For reasons that follow, we conclude that neither of the aggravating factors was proved. This being so, the penalty phase was conducted without legal foundation and the resulting death sentences must be vacated. Defendant's guilt for intentional murder, however, was proved beyond a reasonable doubt, and we therefore reduce defendant's conviction to murder in the second degree and remit the case to the trial court for resentencing.

In early April 1998, defendant and his wife, Jill, signed a separation agreement but continued to live under the same roof at their home in Spafford, Onondaga County. On April 21, during a pre-dawn heated argument, defendant struck Jill repeatedly on the head with a baseball bat. The couple's two young children were nearby and Jill called out, urging them to call the police because their father was trying to kill her. After the attack, defendant phoned his parents for help. They soon arrived at the Cahill residence, along with defendant's brother and a family friend who was a physician. Having been summoned to the scene, the police found Jill lying on the kitchen floor. She was covered in blood, writhing in pain and moaning incoherently. Her left temple was indented from the injury.

Defendant and victim were taken to different hospitals. After hospital personnel treated defendant for minor injuries, the police brought him to the stationhouse for questioning. At first, he stated that Jill had instigated the argument and attacked him with a knife, causing some cuts and scratches on his body. He claimed he struck her in self-defense. Defendant later admitted that he struck Jill with the bat when she was unarmed and that he cut himself, making it look like self-defense. Defendant added that after the assault, he taped a length of garden hose to the tailpipe of his car in order to poison himself with carbon monoxide, but decided against suicide when he saw a rosary in his vehicle.

In June 1998, a grand jury indicted defendant for assault in the first degree and criminal possession of a weapon in the fourth degree. In the months that followed, he and his attorney prepared for trial. In the meantime, there were custody proceedings in Onondaga Family Court, which placed the children with their maternal grandparents and aunt. In addition, Family Court and Onondaga County Court issued orders of protection prohibiting defendant from seeing his children or entering University Hospital, where Jill was confined....

On October 27, 1998, after the hospital was closed to visitors, defendant entered the premises, in disguise. According to several members of the staff, defendant wore a wig and glasses, posing as a maintenance worker, complete with a mop and falsified name tag. Shortly after 10:00 pm, a nurse detected a strong odor in the room and saw Jill having trouble breathing. The nurse also observed a waxy-looking substance on Jill's chest and that Jill's hospital gown caused a burning sensation when touched. Despite efforts to revive her, Jill died the next morning. She had been poisoned. An autopsy revealed that potassium cyanide was administered through her mouth or feeding tube. Police promptly arrested defendant for Jill's murder.

On November 19, 1998, while the assault charges were pending, a grand jury indicted defendant on two counts of first degree murder ....One murder count charged defendant with having murdered Jill to prevent her from testifying against him at his trial for the April 1998 assault (Penal Law 125.27[1][a][v]), the other with intentionally murdering Jill in the course of and in furtherance of a burglary (Penal Law 125.27[1][a][vii]). The grand jury also indicted defendant on two counts of murder in the second degree, burglary in the second degree, aggravated criminal contempt and criminal possession of a weapon in the fourth degree....

Pursuant to CPL 400.27, the court conducted the jury trial in two phases. In the first phase, the jury found defendant guilty of both counts of first degree murder, first degree assault (based on the April 1998 beating) and related charges. The penalty phase followed, in which the jury returned with verdicts of death under both first degree murder counts....

[D]efendant was convicted under Penal Law 125.27(1)(a)(vii). That section elevates intentional murder to capital-eligible murder when a defendant with "intent to cause the death of another person * * * causes the death of such person * * * and * * * the victim was killed while the defendant was in the course of committing or attempting to commit and in furtherance of * * * burglary in the first or second degree * * *." As a matter of statutory interpretation, we conclude that the conviction cannot stand because the burglary carried no intent other than to commit the murder.

Penal Law 125.27(1)(a)(vii) is best understood in light of the Legislature's purpose in devising aggravating factors as predicates for the death penalty....The Legislature drew up a list of aggravating factors to create a subclass of defendants who, in contrast to others who commit intentional murder, it thought deserving of the death penalty. By this device, the lawmakers saw to it that the death penalty could not fall randomly on all murder defendants. The Legislature's factors govern the discretion of courts and juries by limiting capital punishment to certain enumerated categories of intentional killings, ensuring that the state follows its "constitutional responsibility to tailor and apply its law in a manner that avoids the arbitrary and capricious infliction of the death penalty" (Godfrey v. Georgia, 446 U.S. 420, 428 [1980]).

Penal Law 125.27(1) identifies death-eligible defendants as those who commit intentional murders in the context of one or more of 13 aggravating factors. Five aggravating factors relate to the killing of a member of a specific group (police officers, peace officers, corrections employees, witnesses and judges ¶i-iii, v, xii]), two relate to the present or past circumstances of the offender (defendants serving life sentences and defendants previously convicted for murder [¶iv, ix]), four address the circumstances of the killing or criminal transaction (murder committed in furtherance of certain enumerated felonies, multiple murders as part of the same criminal transaction, murder by torture and terrorism [¶vii, viii, x, xiii]). The remaining two involve contract killing and serial murder [¶vi, xi).

Among other arguments, defendant contends that he cannot be convicted under Penal Law 125.27(1)(a)(vii) because the statute requires that the underlying felony (here, burglary in the second degree) have an objective apart from the intentional murder and that the burglary was merely an act that enabled the murder, one of many anticipatory steps along the way.

By the terms of the indictment, defendant was charged with having killed his wife "in the course of committing or attempting to commit and in the furtherance of the crime of Burglary in the Second Degree." Because our analysis turns on whether defendant's burglary qualifies as an aggravating factor, we must address the crime of burglary in the setting before us....

There can be no burglary unless the trespasser intends to commit a separate crime when entering or remaining unlawfully in a building (see People v. Gaines, 74 N.Y.2d 358 [1989]). Burglary is thus an aggravated form of criminal trespass, in which the aggravating factor is the trespasser's intent to commit a separate crime (see People v. Henderson, 41 N.Y.2d 233 [1976]).

With that in mind, we may better appreciate how burglary fits into the design of Penal Law 125.27(1)(a)(vii). The statute begins by declaring that every first degree murder must include an intentional (second degree) murder. An additional aggravating factor—murder "plus"—raises the crime to murder in the first degree. A candidate for first degree murder is the burglar who enters a dwelling to steal or rob or rape and in addition kills someone intentionally, in the course and furtherance of the burglary. It is this double crime—murder "plus"—that is the defining core of Penal Law 125.27(1)(a) and renders the offender eligible for the death penalty.

The case before us does not fit this statutory paradigm. Burglary requires an intent to commit a crime in the burglarized premises, and here the prosecutor uses defendant's "intent to kill" to satisfy the burglary definition. But the very same *Mens rea*—the intent to kill—also defines intentional murder (Penal Law 125.25). Thus, the prosecution employs the identical *mens rea* both to define burglary and to elevate defendant's intentional murder to murder in the first degree. The defense argues that this circularity is impermissible and that the capital murder statute contemplates a felonious intent independent of the murder itself. We agree.

A burglar who intends, for example, both to rob and murder is committing two crimes, both felonies, whose intents are purposively independent of each other. The robbery may be committed in connection with the murder, but as a substantive crime it is distinct from the murder and can be aptly characterized as an aggravating factor that fulfills Penal Law 125.27(1)(a)(vii). It is the "plus" (in the "murder plus" formulation) that is necessary to make it a death-eligible crime.

Burglary, however, is different because it is a trespass—a misdemeanor—that becomes a felony only if the trespasser intends to commit a separate crime when entering a building. If the burglar intends only murder, that intent cannot be used both to define the burglary and at the same time bootstrap the second degree (intentional) murder to a capital crime. To do so would not narrow the class of those eligible for the death penalty, but would widen it. In promulgating the list of aggravators, the Legislature did not expressly sweep within Penal Law 125.27 all killings in which the murderer unlawfully entered the victim's home. We decline to imply such an intent, let alone write one into the statute, in the face of the unswerving legislative goal of narrowing rather than expanding the class of defendants eligible for the death penalty. Nor will we, in the absence of legislative intent or expression, have life or death hinge on whether a defendant engaged in conduct that simply enabled the intended murder and had no point of its own. To do so would spurn rather than follow the Legislature's objectives.

In arguing that defendant's burglary satisfies Penal Law 125.27(1)(a)(vii), the prosecutors and our dissenting colleagues rely heavily on People v. Miller (32 N.Y.2d 157 [1973]). They assert that Miller applies and that if we read Penal Law 125.27(1)(a)(vii) as requiring a felony independent of the murder, we will be overruling a body of felony murder jurisprudence that extends back three decades. This is not so. Miller does not govern this case, and the reason is plain: in Miller, the Court interpreted Penal Law 125.25(3), the felony murder statute. Here, we are reviewing not felony murder but Penal Law 125.27(1)(a)(vii), a capital punishment statute directed at those who commit intentional murder, and more....

In contrast to Penal Law 125.27(1), felony murder covers non-intentional killings. The very purpose of the felony murder doctrine is to utilize the underlying felony as a substitute for the defendant's murderous intent and thereby raise an unintentional killing to the level of murder. As we said in People v. Hernandez (82 N.Y.2d 309, 317 [1993]), "The basic tenet of felony murder liability is that the *Mens rea* of the underlying felony is imputed to the participant responsible for the killing. By operation of that legal fiction, the transferred intent allows the law to characterize a homicide, though unintended and not in the common design of the felons, as an intentional killing" (citations omitted).

Penal Law 125.27(1)(a)(vii) borrows language from the felony murder statute, but is critically different because it deals with intentional, not unintentional, killings. The purposes of the capital statute and the felony murder statute are distinct, and the felonies covered by them are not the same. For example, under the felony murder statute, the killing need not be committed by one of the people engaged in the commission of the underlying crime (People v. Hernandez, 82 N.Y.2d 309 [1993]), whereas Penal Law 125.27(1)(a)(vii) does not apply where the defendant's liability is based on someone else's conduct (unless the defendant commanded the murder). Moreover, felony murder liability for the death of a victim has been broadly construed, whereas the Legislature crafted Penal Law 125.27(1)(a) to narrow the class of eligible offenders....The two concepts share certain components but have entirely different objectives and constituents, and were statutorily constructed to reach different types of homicides and different categories of defendants.

[W]e need not and do not determine whether the prosecution is correct in its assertion that defendant killed his wife "in furtherance of" the burglary. It is certain that the converse is true—defendant committed the burglary to further his intent to kill his wife. That being so, the burglary was not meaningfully independent from the murder. Defendant's trespass on the hospital premises was merely a prerequisite to his committing the murder—an enabling measure that had no purpose or substance other than to serve his only goal, to kill his victim.

We are also aware of the dissent's contention that our interpretation could engender results that, on the surface, appear incongruous. The defendant who breaks into a home with the joint intent of killing the occupant and stealing an appliance could, under our interpretation, be death-eligible, but a defendant who breaks into the same home for the sole purpose of killing the occupant would not. This might appear as a surface flaw, but on further analysis the result is fully in keeping with the statutory plan. In the former case, the defendant who burglarizes in order to steal and commits intentional murder would be punished more severely under Penal Law 125.27(1)(a)(vii) for having committed both murder and a burglary intended apart from the murder. This result is neither arbitrary nor unjust, and is more faithful to the Legislature's language and design.

Accordingly, the judgment of Onondaga County Court should be modified by reducing defendant's conviction of two counts of murder in the first degree to one count of murder in the second degree and remitting to that court for resentencing on the second degree murder as well as the remaining counts and, as so modified, affirmed....

MULTIPLE CHOICE QUESTIONS

1. In the Harris case, if the jury believed that the defendant acted under extreme emotional disturbance, the defendant should be convicted of:
   A. Murder in the second degree.
   B. Manslaughter in the first degree.
   C. Manslaughter in the second degree.
   D. Negligent homicide.

2. If a defendant serves as a "lookout" for an accomplice in a robbery and the accomplice, without the consent of the defendant, kills the victim, the defendant could be guilty of:
   A. No homicide charge.
   B. Murder in some degree.
   C. Manslaughter in the first degree.
   D. Robbery.

3. A defendant who causes a death through her reckless conduct should be guilty of:
   A. Manslaughter in the first degree.
   B. Manslaughter in the second degree.
   C. Criminally negligent homicide.
   D. None of the above.

4. A defendant who intentionally kills a victim may be found guilty of:
   A. Murder in the first degree.
   B. Murder in the second degree.
   C. Manslaughter in the first degree.
   D. All the above.

5. In the Harris case above, the court held that:
   A. The defendant should have been permitted to testify about his extreme emotional disturbance.
   B. The trial judge should have given the jury instructions on how to view extreme emotional disturbance.
   C. The prosecutor should not have been permitted to argue against extreme emotional disturbance.
   D. None of the above.

6. In New York, a defendant can be charged with homicide for killing an unborn child if—
    A. The defendant is the father of the child and gives the mother of the child money to get an abortion during the first trimester of the pregnancy.
    B. The defendant is driving a car and hits a pedestrian and breaks her leg; the pedestrian turns out to be in her eighth month of pregnancy, and has a miscarriage as a result of the traffic accident.
    C. The defendant is responsible for the death of a fetus at any stage of a pregnancy.
    D. All of the above.
    E. None of the above.

7. In the Cahill case above, the court held that:
    A. The defendant should have been convicted of felony murder.
    B. The defendant should have been convicted of first degree murder because he had the intent to kill his wife.
    C. The defendant should have been subject to the death penalty because he had the intent to kill his wife.
    D. The defendant should have been convicted of "murder plus."
    E. None of the above.

8. In the Cahill case above, the court discusses how New York's death penalty statute applies to a person who breaks into a home in order to kill someone, and how it applies to a person who breaks into a home without planning to kill someone, but who decides to kill the homeowner when the homeowner discovers his presence. Which of the following is a correct summary of the court's holding?
    A. A person who breaks into a home in order to kill someone will be treated more severely than someone who forms the intent to kill after breaking into the home.
    B. A person who breaks into a home intending to kill someone will be treated less severely than someone who forms the intent to kill after breaking into the home.
    C. Both crimes will be treated identically under New York's death penalty statute.
    D. None of the above.

DISCUSSION QUESTIONS

1. In the Harris case, why did the defendant not raise an insanity (that is, mental disease or defect) defense?

2. If you were a juror, would you find that Harris acted under extreme emotional disturbance? Why or why not?

3. If you were a prosecutor in the Harris case, would you consider asking the court to dismiss the murder charge and allow the defendant to plead guilty to manslaughter in the first degree? Why or why not?

4. Do you believe that defendants should be able to use the extreme emotional disturbance defense only in situations involving sexual affairs of their spouses, or in any situation?

5. In one case that the Harris court cites, the defendant was allowed to claim extreme emotional disturbance after decapitating someone. What evidence or social policy would merit submitting such a claim to a jury?

6. What are some arguments that could be made to explain why felony murder should not be a strict liability crime?

7. Why is it that only some states make "fetal homicide" a crime? What are the arguments against making it a crime to kill an unborn child? What are the arguments that killing an unborn child should only be a crime in the later stages of a pregnancy?

8. In the Cahill case, the New York Court of Appeals discusses the intent of the New York legislature when it enacted the New York death penalty statute. Can you explain the Court's understanding of the legislators' intent? Do you think the New York legislators intend for the death penalty to apply in cases like Cahill?

Chapter Nine

Crimes against Persons II: Criminal Sexual Conduct, Assault, and Kidnapping

Introduction

In addition to homicide, there are several crimes that involve a violation of a victim's body. The most prominent of these is sexual assault, but these crimes also include simple assault and kidnapping. In addition, in New York, there are several variations of these crimes, such as vehicular assault, gang assault, menacing, hazing, and stalking (all of which can be found in article 120.00 of the Penal Law); and unlawful imprisonment, custodial interference, and coercion (all of which can be found in article 135.00 of the Penal Law). Regardless of how these crimes are characterized, all of them involve circumstances where a victim, because of the conduct of the defendant, suffers an injury, endures sexual contact, or is intimidated or restrained from moving to a location of her or his choosing. This chapter discusses simple assault, sexual assault or rape, and kidnapping.

Simple Assault

A simple assault is the most basic violation of a person's body in that a defendant engages in some conduct that causes the victim to suffer a physical injury. Depending on the state, a simple assault can be termed "assault," "assault and battery," or "battery." New York uses the term "assault," which it defines as (1) intent to (2) cause (3) physical injury to another person, assuming, or course, that the physical injury results (Penal Law 120.00(1)).

New York's Penal Law contains many different types of assaults (Article 120.00), which are based on many factors. Assaults are classified and punished differently based on the mental state with which the defendant acted (intentionally, recklessly, or negligently); the injury sustained by the victim; the status of the victim (such as a police officer or firefighter); and whether the defendant used a weapon in the course of the assault. For example, the most serious type of assault would be one in which the defendant used a deadly weapon to intentionally cause serious physical injury to the victim (Penal Law 120.10(1)), which would be punishable by up to 25 years in prison (Penal Law 70.00(2)(b)).

In the Garcia case below, examine what facts led to the jury's finding that the defendant recklessly, but not intentionally, assaulted the victim.

People v. Garcia, 194 A.D.2d 1011, 599 N.Y.S.2d 669 (3rd Department 1993)

Defendant was convicted upon a jury verdict of assault in the third degree and criminal possession of a weapon in the third degree stemming from his conduct in the early morning hours of August 26, 1990 in causing lacerations to the throat and arm of Douglas

Virgil by striking him with a large broken beer glass. The incident occurred in an apartment at the Olcott Hotel in the City of Oneida, Madison County, and was witnessed by Alan Rossi (the tenant), John Francis and Matthew Francis. The testimony showed that all those present except Matthew Francis had been drinking beer and that while the group was socializing, defendant and Virgil collided and a confrontation between them ensued with punches exchanged until Rossi broke up the fight and defendant left at Rossi's request. Defendant returned within minutes carrying a large beer glass, broke the glass against a doorframe and swiped at Virgil with the broken edge of the glass, ultimately cutting Virgil's throat and arm. The two wrestled to the floor and defendant thereafter departed.

Defendant was acquitted of assault in the second degree (Penal Law 120.05 [2] [intentional assault]) and the lesser included offense of assault in the third degree (Penal Law 120.00 [1]), but convicted of assault in the third degree (Penal Law 120.00 [2] reckless assault]), which was also submitted as a lesser included offense, and criminal possession of a weapon in the third degree (Penal Law 265.02 [1]).

Defendant's first point on appeal is that his conviction for criminal possession of a weapon in the third degree was repugnant to his acquittal on the two intentional assault counts submitted to the jury. We disagree. As to the assault counts on which defendant was acquitted (Penal Law 120.05 [2]; 120.00 [1]), the jury was properly charged that the mental element of both crimes is an intent to cause physical injury. The jury was likewise correctly instructed that the mental element of criminal possession of a weapon in the third degree (Penal Law 265.02 [1]) is "intent to use [the weapon] unlawfully against another." There is no inconsistency between the acquittals on the intentional assault charges and the conviction for weapons possession, because one can intend to use a weapon unlawfully against another, e.g., to commit the crime of menacing (Penal Law 120.15), without necessarily intending to inflict physical injury on that person. Thus, the counts on which defendant was acquitted did not share a common element with the count on which he was convicted, and there is no inherent inconsistency in the verdicts.

Defendant additionally contends that the jury's verdict was against the weight of the evidence and not supported by legally sufficient evidence. Viewing the evidence in a light most favorable to the People and weighing the relative probative force of the testimony and giving deference to the jury's verdict, we conclude that the People met their burden of proving defendant's guilt beyond a reasonable doubt and the verdict was not against the weight of the evidence. All of the eyewitnesses testified that defendant was the aggressor and used the broken glass to cut Virgil. Although some of the witnesses may have been under the influence of alcohol, the jury was aware of this and it was within the jury's province to credit their testimony. According the jury's credibility determinations the deference to which they are entitled, we conclude that there is no basis on which to disturb the jury's finding of guilt.

We have reviewed defendant's remaining contentions, including his claim that the sentence imposed was harsh and excessive, and conclude that they are without merit. Ordered that the judgment is affirmed.

Sexual Assault and Rape

Sexual assault may be thought of as a type of simple assault involving particular parts of the bodies of a defendant and a victim. However, theoretically at least, it is possible that a non-consensual sexual assault might not involve "physical injury" to the victim, as that term is defined in New York (Penal Law 10.00(9)). Thus, sexual assault statutes begin by focusing on prohibiting a defendant from contacting (or touching) another person's sexual or intimate parts for the purpose of sexual gratification (Penal Law 130.00(3)). The "sexual parts" of victims' bodies are usually the penis, anus, mouth, vulva (Penal Law 130.00(2)), and vagina (Penal Law 130.00(1)). Thus, when a defendant initiates, without consent, any contact with another person's sexual parts, the defendant should be guilty of what is termed a "sex offense" under article 130 of the Penal Law. Although the New York sex offense statutes do not explicitly contain a mental state element, in almost all cases, the mental state element should be "intent." Examine the Aronsen case below and analyze why intent should be read into the statutes.

People v. Aronsen, 204 A.D.2d 470, 611 N.Y.S.2d 901 (2nd Department 1994)

Appeal by defendant from a judgment of the Supreme Court, Kings County (Beldock, J.), rendered June 5, 1992, convicting him of sexual abuse in the first degree, upon a jury verdict, and imposing sentence. [T]he judgment is reversed, on the law, and a new trial is ordered. No questions of fact have been raised or considered.

On July 11, 1990, at around midnight, the complaining witness received a visit from her friend, Stewy, who introduced her to the defendant. The complaining witness recognized the defendant, having encountered him several times in the neighborhood. She allowed him to enter into her apartment along with Stewy. While the complaining witness was engaged in a brief conversation with Stewy, she observed the defendant consume the seven or eight large cans of beer which he had brought with him. She observed him consume this quantity of beer, or so she testified, within the space of 10 minutes.

Shortly thereafter, the complaining witness expressed a desire for a roast beef sandwich and stated that one could be purchased at a food store near her apartment. However, she first needed to make a cash withdrawal from an automatic teller machine at a bank located across the street from the food store. The defendant offered to accompany her to that location. The defendant and the complaining witness arrived at the bank and between 12:33 and 12:43 a.m. The complaining witness made several unsuccessful attempts to withdraw the necessary cash. The defendant then suggested that the complaining witness accompany him on a visit to the home of one of his friends. It was on the way to this destination that the defendant allegedly assaulted the complaining witness.

[T]he defendant was accused of several crimes, including rape in the first degree and sodomy in the first degree. At trial, his attorney requested an intoxication charge and this request was denied. The defendant was found guilty of only one count, that is, sexual abuse in the first degree (see Penal Law 130.65[1]), based on evidence of his having forcibly come into contact with the victim's breast for the purpose of sexual gratification. This appeal followed.

The defendant is not guilty of the crime of sexual abuse in the first degree as charged in the indictment unless he acted with the intent to obtain sexual gratification for himself or for the victim (see Penal Law 130.65[1] [based on contact by forcible compulsion with victim's breast]; Penal Law 130.00[3]). As a general rule, evidence of intoxication is relevant only when it bears on the defendant's capacity to form some culpable mental state which constitutes an essential element of the crime charged (see People v Westergard, 69 NY2d 642, 511 N.Y.S.2d 587, 503 N.E.2d 1018). In evaluating whether the jury ought to be instructed as to the significance of evidence relating to intoxication, the trial court must examine the evidence in a light most favorable to the defendant. Applying these general rules, we conclude that an intoxication charge was warranted in the present case.

It is readily apparent that a rational juror might reasonably have concluded that the defendant's inhibitions were reduced or destroyed and that his conduct was consequently altered on account of alcohol consumption. This alone, of course, would not constitute a defense to the crime charged. The fact that his past consumption of alcohol might have weakened or destroyed the defendant's inhibitions against committing a culpable act is irrelevant; his intoxication is relevant only to the extent that it destroyed or weakened his ability to form the culpable mental state which, when associated with such act, gives rise to criminal liability.

The key question, then, is whether a rational juror might have either ascribed the defendant's lewd act to some purpose other than that of achieving sexual gratification (see Penal Law 130.00[3]) or found that the defendant was so besotted as to have had no purpose at all for his engaging in this act. As unlikely as such conclusions might seem to us as a matter of fact, we cannot say, as a matter of law, that they are conclusions which no rational juror could possibly reach. We are therefore obligated to order a new trial. We have examined the defendant's remaining contentions to the extent necessary in light of this disposition, and find them to be without merit.

The sexual offenses in article 130 of New York's Penal Law initially can create confusion, because they encompass many different terms, such as "sexual misconduct," "rape," "sodomy," and "sexual abuse." Nonetheless, the statutes can be read as classifying certain types of sexual contact. For example, the statutes on rape cover prohibited types of sexual intercourse involving penis and vaginal contact (Penal Law 135.35(1)). The statutes on sodomy cover prohibited types of other sexual contact involving penis/anus, penis/mouth, or mouth/anus contact (Penal Law 130.50(1); Penal Law 130.00(2)). [Until it was repealed on February 1, 2001, Penal Law 130.38 made it a B misdemeanor to engage in consensual sodomy, which includes essentially any type of consensual sexual activity between unmarried persons, except for sexual intercourse. The United States Supreme Court struck down a similar Texas law as unconstitutional in the case of Lawrence v.

Texas, 539 U.S. 558 (2003). The Lawrence case would probably have invalidated the New York statute, had it not been repealed.]

Kidnapping

Kidnapping and related crimes are designed to ensure that persons can move about freely. This means that persons should not be forced to go to any location or be prevented from going to any location of their choosing (Penal Law 135.00-135.30). Thus, the Penal Law (article 135) contains statutes designed to prevent unlawful imprisonment, kidnapping, and custodial interference. All these crimes include an element of forcing a person to be in a place where he or she does not want to be (or in the case of a child involved in a custody dispute, taking a child to a place where the child is not authorized to be).

Unlawful imprisonment involves simply restraining a person against her or his will, such as holding a person on the ground. Kidnapping is also a type of restraint, except that it is far more serious. Kidnapping involves abducting a person, taking her to a place where she will not be found, or holding a person for ransom. Such restraints frequently place the victim at risk of great harm. Custodial interference is usually at issue when parents are in the midst of a separation, divorce, or a significant dispute. In violation of a court order, for example, one parent will take a child to another state so that the other parent cannot have contact with the child. The most frequent types of unlawful restraint are unlawful imprisonment and kidnapping, and they usually accompany an additional crime, such as simple assault, sexual assault, or robbery.

Analyze the Tillman case below, and determine why one act of the defendant involved kidnapping and another act involved only unlawful restraint.

People v. Tillman, 69 A.D.2d 975, 416 N.Y.S.2d 102 (4th Department 1979)

Judgment unanimously modified, on the law and facts, and, as modified, affirmed, and defendant remanded to Erie County Supreme Court for resentence, in accordance with the following memorandum: At approximately 12:30 a.m. on September 24, 1976, complainant in the course of parking her car in front of her home was forced at shotgun point by a person whom she identified as the defendant to unlock her car door and admit him and two other youths. With a shotgun and pistol trained on her, she drove under the command of defendant to various locations and was later forced to permit one of the youths to drive the vehicle. Subsequently, she was ordered to retake the wheel and after the two youths exited the vehicle, she was compelled by defendant to drive to a parking lot. There under threat of an exposed razor he raped her. Then approximately 45 minutes after the initial abduction, defendant forced her at shotgun point into the trunk of her automobile, where she was locked and held for approximately 12 hours. After the automobile crashed into a tree and the driver fled, she banged on the trunk lid to attract attention and was finally released.

100

Defendant was convicted of two counts of kidnapping (one related to the restraint imposed upon the complainant before her rape and the second to her confinement and transportation in the trunk of her automobile), one count of rape in the first degree and one count of unauthorized use of a motor vehicle. Defendant contends…(1) that since complainant's confinement was not for ransom but merely incidental to the unlawful taking and use of the automobile, the facts on which the kidnapping counts were predicated did not rise to the level of " kidnapping" in its commonly accepted sense as construed by the courts, and (2) that the trial court erroneously refused to charge unlawful imprisonment as a lesser included offense of the kidnapping counts.

In People v Cassidy (40 NY2d 763, 767), the court stated: "The merger doctrine * * * preclude[s] conviction for kidnapping based on acts which are so much the part of another substantive crime that the substantive crime could not have been committed without such acts and that independent criminal responsibility may not fairly be attributed to them." We hold that the defendant's conviction of kidnapping for the restraint imposed upon complainant before the rape and until her imprisonment in the car's trunk cannot stand. The evidence is clear that the abduction was the incidental means employed to facilitate the commission of the underlying crime of rape. This first incident did not last longer than 45 minutes and the acts upon which the kidnapping count was based were entwined with the commission of the crime of rape. The rape could not have been committed without these acts, and independent criminal responsibility may not be attributed to them. Defendant's acts lack a genuine "kidnapping" aura and do not rise to the level of culpability to constitute kidnapping. However, this does not result in a dismissal of the charge since the crime of unlawful imprisonment was established beyond a reasonable doubt and the judgment should be modified accordingly.

This doctrine, however, does not apply to the count of kidnapping related to complainant's imprisonment in the trunk of her car. This abduction was not necessary for the commission of the rape. She was forced at shotgun point into the trunk after the crime of rape was completed and was not released from its confines for many hours. This kidnapping count is not based on acts which are so much a part of the crime of rape that the rape could not have been committed without them. Moreover, these acts bore no relationship to the unauthorized use by the defendant of complainant's motor vehicle. The court did not err in refusing to charge unlawful imprisonment as a lesser included offense. Although Unlawful imprisonment in the first degree (Penal Law 135.10) is a lesser included offense of kidnapping in the second degree (Penal Law 135.20), there is no "reasonable view of the evidence" under which it could be found that the defendant committed unlawful imprisonment but did not commit kidnapping in the second degree. It is "only where there is some basis in the evidence for finding the accused innocent of the higher crime, and yet guilty of the lower one," that submission of an included crime is justified.

The testimony of complainant that she was abducted by the use and threatened use of deadly physical force, raped and then secreted in the trunk of her car was neither impeached nor contradicted. Her testimony was unequivocal and uncontroverted, except for her identification of defendant, and clearly established kidnapping in the second degree.

Other contentions raised by defendant have been considered and found to be without merit. Accordingly, the judgment convicting defendant of kidnapping in the second degree for the restraint imposed upon complainant before the rape and until her imprisonment in the trunk of the automobile is modified, on the law and facts, by reducing it to a conviction of unlawful imprisonment in the first degree, and, as so modified, the judgment is affirmed. The case is remitted to the Erie County Supreme Court Criminal Trial Term for sentencing upon the unlawful imprisonment conviction.

MULTIPLE CHOICE QUESTIONS

1. The crime of assault (Penal Law 120.00(1)) has as one element:
    A. Touching of the victim.
    B. Physical injury to the victim.
    C. Serious physical injury to the victim.
    D. None of the above.

2. Forcible sodomy has as one element non-consensual:
    A. Kissing.
    B. Sexual intercourse.
    C. Anal intercourse.
    D. All the above.

3. In the Tillman case above, the "merger doctrine" means that:
    A. Two defendants can be convicted of rape and kidnapping.
    B. Two defendants cannot be convicted of rape and kidnapping.
    C. One defendant can be convicted of kidnapping and an accompanying crime.
    D. One defendant cannot be convicted of kidnapping and an accompanying crime.

4. In the Aronsen case, what defense did the defendant raise?
    A. Coercion.
    B. Age.
    C. Consent.
    D. None of the above.

5. From the Garcia case, one can determine that assault contains which of the following mental state elements?
    A. Strict liability.
    B. Recklessness.
    C. Depraved indifference.
    D. Premeditation.

DISCUSSION EXERCISES

1. Should defendants who are convicted of both rape and kidnapping surrounding the same incident receive concurrent or consecutive sentences for the two crimes?

2. The defendant in the Garcia case had swiped a broken bottle at the victim; some time later during the fight, the victim was injured. Once the defendant had exhibited a mental state of intent, how could the jury find him not guilty of the crime of intentional assault?

3. In the Aronsen case, the defendant claimed that his intoxication prevented him from committing sexual abuse upon the complaining witness. Was the defendant arguing that he could not form the intent to commit sexual abuse? Should it matter whether he intentionally committed sexual abuse? If a defendant commits a sexual assault, should he not be guilty regardless of his mental state?

4. In the Tillman case, the court decided that the physical restraint of the victim of a rape is incidental to the rape, and thus cannot be considered kidnapping. Is the court's decision logically defensible? Does rape always involve both restraint and force, thereby justifying convictions for both kidnapping and rape? In finding that kidnapping cannot be part of forcible rape, is the court engaged in legislating?

5. In the New York Penal Law, find the statute that deals with what is usually termed "statutory rape" (130.25(2)). How does the issue of the defendant's mental state affect whether the defendant will be convicted?

6. What are the policy reasons behind creating a crime titled "custodial interference"?

7. What are the key differences between kidnapping and unlawful imprisonment?

Chapter Ten

Crimes against Habitation: Burglary and Arson

Introduction

The purpose of many criminal statutes is to protect private property such as money, stocks and bonds, and automobiles. The two most serious types of property crimes, however, are burglary and arson, which involve significant invasions of places people go for shelter, peace of mind, and their livelihood, such as their homes and workplaces. Moreover, in addition to the damage to property and privacy that burglary and arson can cause, they also create a significant risk that someone will be harmed in the course of a burglary or arson. Generally speaking, burglary statutes apply to unlawful invasions of shelters, such as buildings and homes. Arson statutes apply to the destruction of those places, as well as automobiles, through fire.

Burglary

Burglary is a crime in which a defendant (1) knowingly (2) enters (3) a building or dwelling with the (4) intent to commit a crime inside. In New York and most states, the degree of burglary for which a defendant will be responsible depends on the type of place that the defendant entered. "Dwellings," which are buildings where people sleep at night, receive more statutory protection than other "buildings," which are structures that include offices, warehouses, schools, and even enclosed trucks (Penal Law 140.00(2-4)). For example, if a defendant enters a warehouse to steal electronics equipment, he would be guilty of burglary in the third degree (Penal Law 140.20), a D felony punishable by up to 7 years in prison (Penal Law 70.00(2)(d)). If the defendant entered a dwelling, such as a house or an apartment, to steal electronics equipment, he would be guilty of burglary in the second degree (Penal Law 140.25(2)), a C felony punishable by up to 15 years in prison (Penal Law 70.00(2)(c)).

The crime of burglary is often self-evident. When a defendant is inside a dwelling or building when no one but the occupants should be there, the main issue to be determined is only "what was on the defendant's mind." If the defendant is inside someone else's home at 2:00 a.m., having gained entry through cutting a window silently with a special tool used frequently by burglars (Penal Law 130.45), the police may infer that the person inside intended to steal something and is thus a "burglar." [Note that a burglar is someone who intends to commit a crime inside a building or dwelling, but a robber is someone who forcibly takes property from a person.]

People v. Barney, 99 N.Y.2d 367, 786 N.E.2d 31, 756 N.Y.S.2d 132(2003)

On August 21, 1999, the only occupant of the subject premises died in a motorcycle accident. Aware of the death and that decedent kept marijuana in the house, defendant entered the house through an unlocked door and proceeded to search for the drugs. Unable to locate the marijuana, defendant began to gather other property found in the house when the police, summoned by a neighbor, came and arrested him. At the time, the utilities were still connected and the house was furnished. Although the house was owned by decedent's mother, she maintained a separate residence and had no intention of moving in. After her son's death and prior to the burglary she had given a key to her son's friend so that he could take care of the premises.

Defendant was indicted for second degree burglary and attempted petit larceny. At trial, the court denied defendant's request to submit the lesser included offenses of burglary in the third degree or criminal trespass in the third degree to the jury, and denied defendant's motion to dismiss the charge of second degree burglary on the ground of insufficient evidence. Defendant was subsequently convicted of burglary in the second degree and attempted petit larceny.

At common law the crime of burglary consisted exclusively of breaking into a dwelling-place at night. Burglary of a dwelling at night involved not only great alarm to its occupants but also increased likelihood of injury to an occupant attempting to defend hearth and home. Early revisions of the Penal Law recognized varying degrees of burglary and assigned the greater culpability for entering a dwelling at night where a person could be found because of the greater risk of harm associated with such an entry.

Under our current penal statute, a person commits burglary in the second degree when he or she knowingly enters a building with the intent to commit a crime and where factors tending to increase the likelihood of physical injury are present (see Penal Law 140.25[1]) or, as relevant here, the building is a dwelling (see Penal Law 140.25[2]). A "dwelling" is defined as "a building which is usually occupied by a person lodging therein at night" (Penal Law 140.00[3]).

Proof at trial established that the structure was a one-family residence that was fully furnished with working utilities and could have been occupied overnight. Decedent's property was still in the house, including food in the refrigerator. Further, it is undisputed that the house was ordinarily occupied overnight by the decedent before his death. Viewing this evidence in a light most favorable to the People, it is clear that there is a valid line of reasoning by which the jury could have concluded that the house was "usually occupied by a person lodging therein at night."

Even viewing the evidence in a light most favorable to the defendant, it is clear that the structure in question was a furnished residence. It was suitable for human habitation and had been occupied three days prior to the burglary by the decedent. Thus, we conclude that there was no reasonable view of the evidence that the house was not a dwelling within the meaning of the Penal Law, and therefore the trial court properly refused to charge the lesser included offense.

Defendant's remaining contentions are without merit. Accordingly, the order of the Appellate Division should be affirmed.

In the Barney case, the intruder's intent could be inferred from the fact that he was caught by the police stealing property while inside a home where he did not belong. Determining an intruder's intent may not be resolved as easily, however, when the police find a homeless person inside a warehouse at 2:00 a.m. The homeless person may have entered the warehouse with the intent to steal electronics equipment, in which case the homeless person could be considered a burglar. However, if the homeless person entered the warehouse only to sleep there through the night, he had no intent to commit a crime inside. Therefore, he would not be guilty of burglary, although he would be guilty of criminal trespass in the third degree, a B misdemeanor (Penal Law 140.10).

Examine the Grant case, below, which illustrates that the key in proving burglary is showing that the defendant entered a building with the intent to commit a crime inside the building. If the prosecution cannot prove such intent, the defendant should be convicted of trespassing instead of burglary.

People v. Grant, 132 A.D.2d 929, 518 N.Y.S.2d 262 (4th Department 1987)

Judgment unanimously reversed on the law and new trial granted.

Defendant was convicted of burglary in the third degree and grand larceny in the second degree for stealing seven cartons of baseball caps from a trailer atop a flatbed car in the Conrail yard in Niagara Falls. We agree with defendant's contention on appeal that the court erred in denying his request to instruct the jury on trespass as a lesser included offense of burglary in the third degree.

Trespass is a lesser included offense of burglary in the third degree because it is theoretically impossible to commit burglary without concomitantly and by the same conduct committing trespass (Penal Law 140.05, 140.20). Therefore, the court was bound to charge trespass at defendant's request unless there was no reasonable view of the evidence that defendant was guilty of trespass but not of burglary. There was a reasonable view of the evidence in this case that defendant committed trespass but not burglary. Defendant's testimony and statements to police upon his arrest were consistent in maintaining that he merely hopped over the flatbed car in taking a commonly used shortcut through the railroad yard while walking home from a friend's house. Defendant consistently denied that he or an accomplice entered the trailer or stole anything. Thus, while he admitted committing trespass, defendant denied those elements which distinguish burglary in the third degree from that lesser offense, i.e., entry of a building and intent to commit a crime therein (see Penal Law 140.05, 140.20).

The conviction for grand larceny in the second degree must be reversed along with the conviction for burglary. On this record, if defendant were convicted of trespass after retrial on only the burglary charge, that verdict would be inconsistent with the conviction for grand larceny. Since the indictment specifically charged defendant with stealing goods from an enclosed trailer, there would be no basis for the jury to conclude that defendant or his accomplice stole the goods but that they did not unlawfully enter the trailer. In order to obviate the risk of repugnant verdicts, we reverse the entire judgment and direct a retrial on both counts of the indictment.

Arson

The focus of arson statutes in New York (Penal Law article 150) is on preventing the destruction of buildings and automobiles through the use of fire or an incendiary device that causes an explosion. In addition to the arson statutes, there are many other statutes that prohibit the destruction of property. They are contained in article 145 of the Penal Law and include such crimes as criminal mischief (damaging any property), criminal tampering (tampering with property to cause a substantial inconvenience to others), cemetery desecration, and making graffiti. However, arson is a distinct and particularly dangerous property crime, because people frequently occupy the buildings and automobiles that are the targets of arsonists. Also, fire and explosions can harm people in the immediate area of the building or automobile burned by the arsonist, as well as the firefighters and police officers who must deal with the emergencies created by fire and smoke.

A defendant is guilty of arson when he or she (1) intentionally or recklessly (2) damages (3) a building or automobile by (4) starting a fire or causing an explosion (Penal Law 150.05-150.20). While burglary statutes are based on whether the defendant entered a building or dwelling, arson statutes do not distinguish between buildings and dwellings. That is, a burglary of a dwelling is punished more severely than a burglary of a building that is not used as a dwelling. In contrast, arsons of a building, automobile, or dwelling would be punished equally, because arson is a crime that is extremely dangerous wherever it is committed.

Examine the Fleming case, and determine the damage that is necessary to prove arson. Note that the court finds that even the "slightest damage" to a structure can be the basis of an arson conviction. Examine the court's reasoning and determine whether you would reach the same result.

People v. Fleming, 164 A.D.2d 942, 560 N.Y.S.2d 50 (2nd Department 1990)

Appeal by the defendant from a judgment of the Supreme Court, Kings County (Juviler, J.), rendered August 20, 1987, convicting him of attempted murder in the second degree and arson in the fourth degree, after a nonjury trial, and imposing sentence. Ordered that the judgment is affirmed.

The evidence adduced at the trial establishes that a fire was started in the defendant's mother's apartment by putting a match to combustible liquid poured on the mattress at the foot of the bed. Burned clothing was found on the bed after the fire. The fire caused smoke damage to the ceiling and walls, heat damage to a light fixture in the ceiling, and charring to the mattress and bed frame. The evidence also established that the defendant, who was at the apartment at the time the fire started, admitted to neighbors that, because of a dispute with his mother over money, he "just tried to burn the bitch," that he tied her up and set her on fire, and that he "wanted the bitch to die." The defendant's mother, who was conscious after the fire and who had no burns on her body and no thermal injury to her lungs, died in the hospital 10 hours later. According to the prosecution, she died of smoke inhalation, while, according to the defense, her death was the result of a heart attack.

As a result of insufficient proof that the defendant's mother died as a direct result of the fire, the court found the defendant not guilty of murder in the second degree. It nonetheless convicted him of attempted murder in the second degree. It also found him guilty of arson in the fourth degree. The defendant contends on appeal that there was no "damage" to the building so as to support the arson conviction (see Penal Law 150.05 [1]), and that the evidence was inadequate to establish that he intended to cause his mother's death so as to support a conviction for attempted murder in the second degree (see Penal Law 110.00, 125.25 [1]). We disagree.

Viewing the evidence in a light most favorable to the prosecution (see People v Contes, 60 NY2d 620), we find it was legally sufficient to establish the defendant's guilt of both crimes beyond a reasonable doubt. It is not necessary that a building "burn" in order for there to be arson in the fourth degree. The slightest damage to a building caused by a fire which is intentionally set is sufficient to establish the damage element of this crime and the smoke and heat damage did so here. Moreover, the fact that the defendant intended to cause his mother's death may be proven by circumstantial evidence and the trier of fact may infer that the defendant is presumed to have intended the natural and probable consequences of his acts.

The physical evidence together with the defendant's admissions are here sufficient to establish the defendant's intent to kill. Finally, upon the exercise of our factual review power, we are satisfied that the findings of guilt were not against the weight of the evidence.

MULTIPLE CHOICE QUESTIONS

1. In burglary, what is the mental state element with regard to what a guilty defendant had in her mind when she is inside a building or dwelling?
   A. Intent.
   B. Recklessness.
   C. All the above.
   D. None of the above.

2. What is the mental state element(s) for arson?
   A. Intent.
   B. Recklessness.
   C. All the above.
   D. None of the above.

3. What kind of damage must the prosecution prove to obtain an arson conviction?
   A. Smoke damage.
   B. Fire damage.
   C. The threat of fire or smoke damage.
   D. All the above.

4. In the Grant case, what is the underlying alleged crime upon which the burglary prosecution is based?
   A. Breaking and entering.
   B. Grand larceny.
   C. Criminal mischief.
   D. All the above.

5. In New York, which of the following can be burglarized?
   A. Building.
   B. School.
   C. Delivery truck.
   D. All the above.

DISCUSSION QUESTIONS

1. In the Fleming case, above, although the court found the defendant not guilty of intentional murder, what other theory could the prosecution have used to argue for a murder conviction?

2. In the Fleming case, is the court's test for whether arson has occurred, the "slightest damage" test, precise enough to notify persons as to the meaning of arson? For example, if someone holds a lit match close to a building and, thus, causes an infinitesimal part of the building to "smell," is this "slight damage" justifying an arson charge?

3. In burglary cases, should a homeowner be allowed to use deadly force anytime a burglar enters the home?

4. What are the mental state elements in a burglary case, and when must the defendant have them if the defendant is to be found guilty of burglary?

5. Burglary of a dwelling (even if no one is home) with a deadly weapon and robbery with a deadly weapon are both B felonies. Should they both be treated the same? Does the equality of penalties for burglary and robbery reflect a capitalistic society?

6. Would the driver of a car who turned around in a homeowner's driveway be guilty of any crime? Use the Grant case for guidance.

Chapter Eleven

Crimes against Property

Introduction

In a capitalistic society, the government must provide a vast number of rules with which to regulate economic transactions so that people can know how to regulate their behavior to maximize profits. Some "business" transactions are made criminal in capitalistic societies because the transactions damage the free market economy; in other cultures that do not value the free market in the same way, similar behavior may not be a crime. For example, in some cultures it is not illegal for a seller of a worthless painting to claim that the painting was done by Michelangelo to induce a buyer to purchase the painting. In the United States, however, including New York, such a false representation would be a crime if the representation induced the buyer to purchase the painting. Thus, crimes against property can be thought of as unlawful attempts to obtain property of another through lies, deceit, false representations, and force.

Although a crime against property can include the destruction of someone else's property (see Penal Law article 145), the focus of this chapter is on crimes that are committed to obtain someone else's property for the benefit of the defendant. In New York, the Penal Law contains many statutes designed to protect property. Article 155, titled "Larceny," prohibits a number of methods by which to take property of another person. Article 155 includes prohibitions on crimes popularly known as "stealing," "embezzlement," and "extortion." Article 158 of the Penal Law prohibits "Welfare Fraud." Article 160 prohibits robbery. Article 165 prohibits thefts and unauthorized uses of automobiles, as well as the possession of stolen property. Article 170 prohibits forgery. This chapter will focus on larceny, robbery, embezzlement, extortion, fraud and false pretenses.

Larceny

Larceny is stealing. A larceny will be converted into a robbery when the defendant uses force (or the threat of it) to steal property from a person. The basic elements of larceny or stealing are the (1) intent (2) to take (3) another person's property (4) without her permission so as to (5) deprive her of the property permanently. The Penal Law contains many types of larcenies to cover a wide variety of circumstances in which a victim's property is taken. Sometimes the types of larcenies are distinguished in part by the value of the property that is taken. A candy bar costs less than a large diamond ($1 versus $2,000,000), and, thus, the candy bar thief will be guilty of only "petit larceny," which is the theft of any property (Penal Law 155.25). The diamond thief will be guilty of "grand larceny in the first degree" if the value of the diamond exceeded $1,000,000 (Penal Law 155.42). The degree of these types of larcenies is determined by the value of the property taken.

The types of larcenies in the Penal Law are also determined by the methods used by the defendant to obtain the property. For example, if a thief steals a candy bar from the shelf of a store, the thief is guilty of only petit larceny, a misdemeanor. However, if the thief steals a candy bar from the hand of another person, the thief will be guilty of "grand larceny in the fourth degree" (Penal Law 155.30(5)), an E felony, for taking property from the person of another. Theft of property from a person is a more serious crime, because a person can be traumatized by the theft, but a store shelf cannot be, and also because there is a risk that the person will be harmed when a thief takes something from her body. In the "candy bar larceny from a person" illustration, it was assumed that the thief did not use "force."

In the following case, People v Bastian, the defendant committed larceny by taking money in exchange for a promise to do something that he could not legally do. Note how the amount of money involved changed the degree of larceny of which he was convicted.

People v. Bastian, 743 N.Y.S.2d 217, 294 A.D.2d 882 (4th Department 2002)

Defendant appeals from a judgment convicting him after a jury trial of scheme to defraud in the first degree (Penal Law 190.65[1][b]) and grand larceny in the fourth degree (155.30[1]). The evidence at trial established that defendant promised two women, one of whom was an undercover officer, that he would make their driving while intoxicated (DWI) charges disappear in exchange for a fee. Defendant contends that the evidence is legally insufficient to support his conviction of both crimes because the People did not establish fraudulent intent or a false promise. We disagree. An "inference of wrongful intent logically flowed from the proven facts and [a] valid line of reasoning could lead a rational trier of fact, viewing the evidence in the light most favorable to the People, to conclude that the defendant committed the charged crime" (People v. Norman, 85 N.Y.2d 609, 620, 627 N.Y.S.2d 302, 650 N.E.2d 1303). Contrary to defendant's further contention, County Court properly admitted evidence of defendant's prior crimes on the issue of defendant's intent to defraud the two victims. See People v Molineux, 168 N.Y. 264, 293-294 ("When fraudulent intent is in issue, evidence of other similar acts [is] admissible to negate the existence of an innocent state of mind").

Defendant further contends that the evidence before the grand jury was legally insufficient to establish that he stole more than $1,000 from one person. It is well settled that, "when a judgment of conviction has been rendered based upon legally sufficient trial evidence, appellate review of a claim alleging insufficiency of Grand Jury evidence is barred" (People v Wiggins, 89 N.Y.2d 872, 874, 653 N.Y.S.2d 91, 675 N.E.2d 845). Here, the People presented legally sufficient evidence at trial to establish that defendant stole more than $1,000 (see Penal Law 155.30[1]). Although defendant promised each victim that he would help her with her DWI charges in exchange for $700 or $800, he collected $1,500 from only the undercover officer on behalf of both victims. Under these circumstances, where the larceny occurred at the same time and place and pursuant to a single intent and common plan, aggregation of the amount taken by defendant was permissible.

It is hereby ordered that the judgment so appealed from be and the same hereby is unanimously affirmed.

Robbery

If in the course of stealing from a person, however, a thief's method is to use or threaten to use force, the crime will be a robbery, not a larceny. The Penal Law contains three types of robberies, which are based on the type of force the defendant uses to obtain property from a person. A defendant would be guilty of "robbery in the third degree" if he pushed the victim during the course of the theft (Penal Law 160.05). The defendant would be guilty of "robbery in the second degree" if he caused a physical injury to the victim while pushing her, a robbery that is essentially a theft plus an assault (Penal Law 160.10(2)(a)). The defendant would be guilty of "robbery in the first degree" if he caused a "serious" physical injury to the victim while pushing her, a robbery that is essentially a theft plus a higher degree of assault (Penal Law 160.15(1)). A robber who is armed with a deadly weapon or who pretends to have a deadly weapon would also be guilty of robbery in the first degree. Thus, Penal Law 160.15(1) covers robberies where the robber, without actually having a gun, puts his hand into his coat pocket and says, "Give me all your money or I'll shoot you."

In the case below, People v. Coleman, the court examines the degree of force necessary to convert a theft into robbery. Even a relatively small amount of force can constitute a robbery, such as pushing the victim aside or striking her, as the Coleman case explains. Also note that under Penal Law 35.15(2)(b), deadly force can used to stop a robbery. In the Coleman case, consider whether New York should sanction the killing of the robber by the cashier of the grocery store.

People v. Coleman, 278 A.D.2d 891, 718 N.Y.S.2d 504 (4th Department 2000)

Judgment unanimously modified on the law and as modified affirmed in accordance with the following Memorandum: Defendant appeals from a judgment convicting him after a nonjury trial of robbery in the third degree (Penal Law 160.05), attempted petit larceny (Penal Law 110.00, 155.25), and two counts of petit larceny (Penal Law 155.25). County Court sentenced defendant as a second felony offender to concurrent terms of imprisonment of 2 to 4 years for the robbery count, one year for each count of petit larceny, and six months for the attempted petit larceny count.

Contrary to defendant's contention, the evidence is legally sufficient to support the robbery conviction. The testimony of the cashier at the grocery store that defendant struck her, causing her to fall, provided the requisite evidence of force to support the robbery conviction. Further, the verdict convicting defendant of robbery in the third degree is not against the weight of the evidence. The determination regarding the credibility of the witnesses is a task within the province of the fact finder, and its judgment should not be lightly disturbed unless clearly unsupported by the record.

We agree with defendant, however, that the sentence imposed for attempted petit larceny is illegal. The maximum permissible sentence for attempted petit larceny, a class B misdemeanor (see Penal Law 110.05 [8]; 155.25), is a definite sentence of imprisonment not to exceed three months (see Penal Law 70.15 [2]). Because the court expressly stated that it was sentencing defendant to the maximum sentence allowed, we modify the judgment by reducing the sentence imposed for attempted petit larceny to a determinate term of imprisonment of three months.

Embezzlement

Another method by which a larceny is committed is called "embezzlement." Embezzlement, containing all the elements of larceny, is the misappropriation of the property of another in situations where the property was initially lawfully in the possession of the embezzler. For example, the term "embezzlement" is often applied to bank employees because they may steal money, bonds, or stocks that were initially entrusted to them. If the bank employee takes home $4000 of a customer's deposit instead of securing the $4000 deposit in the bank's safe, the employee has really committed a "larceny" (Penal Law 155.35), which is the term used in the Penal Law. In popular literature and some jurisdictions, the term "embezzlement" is sometimes used to signify the method of larceny utilized by the bank employee. In New York, embezzlement is simply classified as a type of larceny that is dependent on the value of the property taken.

See the Yannett case below for an illustration of the issues surrounding embezzlement. In Yannett, the main discussion focuses on the status of the money the defendant received from nursing home residents. Whether the defendant committed embezzlement depended on whether he had agreed to hold the money for the residents in trust. Thus, the defendant's criminal liability depended on "the deal" he had made with the nursing home residents.

People v. Yannett, 49 N.Y.2d 296, 401 N.E.2d 410, 425 N.Y.S.2d 300 (1980)

Defendant appeals from an order of the Appellate Division which affirmed a judgment of Broome County Court convicting him of the crime of larceny in the second degree. The conviction is premised upon the claim that defendant embezzled certain funds that were in his possession but were actually owned by certain residents of a nursing home owned and operated by defendant. The dispositive question on this appeal is whether the funds which defendant was convicted of embezzling were held by him on behalf of the residents, or whether those moneys were in fact owned by defendant. For the reasons discussed below, we conclude that defendant was the actual owner of the money in question, although he was otherwise indebted to the residents. Since the mere failure to pay one's debts cannot sustain a conviction for larceny by embezzlement, defendant's conviction must be set aside and the indictment dismissed.

Defendant is the owner-operator of the Endicott Nursing Home. As is true of most such facilities, defendant's nursing home is funded mainly in three ways: payments made by private residents, their families, or some other nongovernmental source; payments from local agencies made pursuant to the State Medicaid program on behalf of needy residents; and payments made by Medicare, the Federal health insurance program, for the care of eligible residents. As a condition to participating in the Medicare program, a nursing home is required to obtain certification from the Federal Government and to enter into a Medicare provider agreement in which it agrees that it will charge those persons eligible for Medicare no more than a set rate established by the Medicare program for that particular home. The home is free, however, to charge private residents a higher rate. Furthermore, Medicare provides the full amount of the Medicare rate for the first 20 days of an eligible person's stay at the home, while for the next 80 days, Medicare pays that rate less a coinsurance charge which the eligible resident is required to pay himself. During that full 100-day period, however, the maximum which a home can charge an eligible resident is limited by the provider agreement to the Medicare rate.

As noted above, when a nursing home applies for participation in the Medicare program, it must first be certified and is then required to enter into a Medicare provider agreement. Moreover, before benefits are paid for a particular resident, that person's eligibility must first be determined by Medicare. All this, of course, may and usually does take considerable time, and in the meanwhile the nursing home needs revenue to operate. The home's solution in such a situation is to require even those residents who seem eligible for Medicare to pay their own way pending approval by Medicare. During this period the home may, and defendant did, charge the higher, private resident rates, rather than the lower Medicare rate.

However, the provider agreement requires the home, upon being notified that a particular person is eligible for Medicare, to refund to that resident the entire amount which the resident had previously paid the home during the period in which he was actually eligible but had not yet been approved, including the difference between the Medicare rate and the higher private resident rate, less the coinsurance charge when applicable. If the payments have been made by someone other than the resident, the refunds are to be made to that person. If the resident has died in the interim, the payments are to be made to the patient's estate, pursuant to State law.

If for some reason the refund cannot be made within 60 days after the nursing home is notified that a particular resident is eligible for Medicare, then the nursing home is required to set aside an amount equal to the refund in a separate account until payment can be made to the proper party. After the nursing home refunds the proper amount to the appropriate person or places it in a separate account if a refund cannot be timely made, then the local Medicare representative (in this State, Blue Cross) reimburses the home at the Medicare rate. It is important to note that under this plan, no payments are required to be made by Medicare to the nursing home until after the nursing home refunds the proper amount to the resident or sets up a separate account when mandated.

In the instant case, the jury by its verdict necessarily found that instead of making full refunds to certain residents as was required by the Medicare agreement, defendant made only partial and in some cases no refunds. During the period prior to Medicare approval of those residents, defendant charged them at the higher private resident rate, as he was apparently allowed to do under the provider agreement. When he was notified that those persons were eligible for Medicare, he was then required by the agreement to refund to them the full amount of the payments they had made to him, less the coinsurance fee for periods after the initial 20 days.

Instead, defendant refunded at most only the amount of the reimbursement payments Medicare was obliged to make to him for those persons, and retained the difference between the higher private resident rate and the Medicare approved rate. This was a clear violation of the provider agreement, which mandated full refunds. Unfortunately, despite defendant's failure to refund the full amount due the residents, Medicare, through its agent Blue Cross, forwarded the Medicare payments to defendant although he was not entitled to any money under the agreement until he made full refunds to the residents. Defendant now stands convicted of larceny in the second degree on the theory that he embezzled funds owned by the residents to whom he did not give full refunds (see Penal Law, 155.05, subd 2, par [a]; 155.35). The Appellate Division affirmed the judgment of conviction, and defendant now appeals to this court. There must be a reversal, since the funds defendant was convicted of embezzling simply were not the property of the residents.

A distinction must be drawn between the refusal to pay a valid debt and the crime of larceny by embezzlement. The essence of the crime of larceny by embezzlement is the conversion by the embezzler of property belonging to another which has been entrusted to the embezzler to hold on behalf of the owner (see Penal Law 155.05, subds 1-2). In the instant case, the money which defendant has been convicted of stealing never belonged to the residents of his nursing home, nor was it entrusted to defendant to hold on behalf of the residents. Although the residents had a contractual right to receive refunds from defendant equal to the full amount they had previously paid him, minus any coinsurance fees, the money from which defendant was required to make those payments belonged to defendant rather than to the residents. Hence, the failure to pay the full refunds did not constitute larceny by embezzlement.

When the residents initially paid the private resident rate to defendant, that money became the defendant's money. It was not given to him in trust, and he was free to use it for any purpose he wished, although he was of course contractually obliged to provide the services which comprised the promised consideration for payment of the fees. The fact that defendant had also assumed an obligation to provide a refund should the residents subsequently be approved for Medicare benefits does not in any way modify the legal conclusion that those funds were the property of defendant and defendant alone. Accordingly, the order appealed from should be reversed and the indictment should be dismissed.

Extortion

Extortion, like embezzlement, is a larceny that contains one additional element. Extortion is a larceny in which the defendant obtains property of the victim by making the victim fear that the defendant/extortionist will injure a person or damage property in the future, or do a number of other acts that will cause the victim to be placed in fear (Penal Law 155.05(2)(e)(i-ix)). Extortion is different from robbery in that it does not contain an "immediate" threat to use force to obtain property from a person. As with embezzlement, the term "extortion" is used by other jurisdictions and in popular culture to denote essentially a unique method of larceny. Under New York Penal Law, however, extortion is simply termed a "grand larceny" in the second (155.40(2)) or fourth (155.30(6)) degree, depending on the type of extortion. For example, a threat to kill the victim in the future if he does not sell his land to the extortionist would be a more serious type of extortion than a threat to publicize a victim's sexual secrets if he did not sell the land.

In the case of People v. Caban, below, a police officer faces a charge of grand larceny for threatening to prosecute a cab driver for not returning money from a wallet that the wallet's owner claimed had been in the wallet when she lost it. As you read the case, decide whether a police officer should face such a charge, when police officers must daily use the threat of force to arrest criminals, investigate crimes, and aid victims. Consider whether the police officer had probable cause to believe that the cab driver took the money.

People v. Caban, 258 A.D.2d 87, 696 N.Y.S.2d 1 (1st Department 1999)

In the words of Grover Cleveland, "a public office is a public trust." This applies not only to elected officials, but to all who work for the people, including the police. Must such a public servant who commits extortion be charged with that crime under the same section of the Penal Law with which a civilian would be charged? Or may the District Attorney charge an officer with a separate count of extortion requiring abuse of his/her public office, a crime which a civilian could not commit? The District Attorney may decide to charge a police officer with violation of the law as a civilian or, if the circumstances warrant, in his/her opinion may charge the officer with the same crime based upon an abuse of police power. A court may not interfere with that discretionary power of the District Attorney and dictate what charges should be brought. "Political theorists since Locke have argued variations on the theory that governmental office is distinct from a property right and represents power held in trust for the citizenry. Thus, the expectations held of public officials are deeply ingrained in our culture, and unfair surprise does not result when the criminal law enforces these expectations."

Defendant is a police officer whose wife took a livery cab operated by one Juan Alvarez and left her purse in the cab. A later passenger found Mrs. Caban's purse in the cab and Mr. Alvarez returned it to her at her home. When he did so, he asked her to "check it out." She "opened it a little bit" and said "it is fine." However, later that evening, Mr. Alvarez was told by his dispatcher to call the 41st Precinct. Upon arriving at the precinct, he was told by Sergeant Caban through an interpreter that $100 was missing from the purse. Sergeant Caban, in police uniform, demanded that the driver return the money. When Mr. Alvarez denied taking the money, defendant allegedly told him he did not want to hear "stories" and if Alvarez did not produce the money, he would put him in a cell. Defendant took money from Alvarez's pocket and counted it. Defendant then allegedly demanded Alvarez's driver's license and taxi license and said if Alvarez did not look for the money, defendant would take the licenses away. Sergeant Caban handcuffed Alvarez behind his back and put him in a cell. Alvarez asked the interpreter, Officer Diaz, what he should do since he was innocent. The officer allegedly told Alvarez to give defendant the money even if it came from his own pocket. After he gave defendant $100, he was allowed to leave the station house.

Defendant Caban was charged with larceny by extortion pursuant to Penal Law 155.40 (2) (c) based on his having instilled fear that he would use or abuse his position as a police officer. The IAS Court dismissed the first count of the indictment charging defendant with grand larceny in the second degree on the ground that the People should have instructed the Grand Jury on the affirmative defense to Penal Law 155.05 (2) (e) (iv). That section defines larceny by extortion as follows: "A person obtains property by extortion when he compels or induces another person to deliver such property to himself or to a third person by means of instilling in him a fear that, if the property is not so delivered, the actor or another will ..."(iv) Accuse some person of a crime or cause criminal charges to be instituted against him." Penal Law 155.15 (2) provides as an affirmative defense: "In any prosecution for larceny by extortion committed by instilling in the victim a fear that he or another person would be charged with a crime, it is an affirmative defense that the defendant reasonably believed the threatened charge to be true and that his sole purpose was to compel or induce the victim to take reasonable action to make good the wrong which was the subject of such threatened charge."

Even if the evidence suggests herein that defendant committed larceny by extortion pursuant to Penal Law 155.05 (2) (e)(iv), namely, by instilling a fear that defendant would accuse the victim Alvarez of a crime or cause criminal charges to be instituted against him, the affirmative defense applicable to that charge was not required to be given to the Grand Jury in this case. The sole extortion charge here was based on Penal Law 155.05 (2) (e) (viii), i.e., instilling fear that defendant would use or abuse his official position as a public servant: "(viii) Use or abuse his position as a public servant by performing some act within or related to his official duties, or by failing or refusing to perform an official duty, in such manner as to affect some person adversely."

The evidence before the Grand Jury showed that defendant instilled fear in Mr. Alvarez by handcuffing him and putting him in a cell. Further, he took away Alvarez's driver's license and taxi license and threatened not to return them if Alvarez did not give him money. Had the People chosen to charge defendant with larceny by extortion based upon defendant's threat to cause charges to be brought against Alvarez, without instructing the Grand Jury on the affirmative defense in question, then dismissal of that charge might have been warranted.

However, the People instead chose to charge defendant with grand larceny based upon the threatened use or abuse of defendant's position as a public official. Having done so, there was no concomitant obligation to instruct the Grand Jury on the affirmative defense which, on its face, is only applicable to "any prosecution for larceny by extortion committed by instilling in the victim a fear that he or another person would be charged with a crime" (Penal 155.15 [2]). Accordingly, the order of the Supreme Court, entered on or about June 30, 1998, which dismissed the first count of the indictment should be reversed to the extent appealed from, on the law, the first count of the indictment reinstated and the matter remanded for further proceedings.

Fraud and False Pretenses

People use a multitude of illegal methods to obtain the property of others. Defendants who commit the crimes discussed above (larceny, robbery, embezzlement, and extortion) obtain property without the consent of the owner. With regard to fraud and false pretenses, defendants obtain property with the consent of the owner by lying. For example, under articles 158 and 176 of the Penal Law, a defendant commits "welfare fraud" or "insurance fraud" by claiming he is another person so that he can collect the benefits to which that other person was entitled. Similarly, a person can be guilty of "forgery" under article 170 of the Penal Law for falsely completing, altering, or making documents and written instruments, such as wills, identification cards, and money. The essence of these types of crimes is that the defendant has intentionally said, written, or otherwise done something to create a false impression in the mind of another person to induce that person to give particular property to the defendant—property to which the defendant is not entitled.

In People v. Sala, the case below, the defendants are charged with grand larceny. The theory of the prosecution's case is that the defendants obtained property through false pretenses—that is, they concealed a material fact. Read the court's decision and determine whether a grand larceny conviction, based on a theory of false pretenses, must rest on false statements affirmatively made by a defendant or on the defendants' failure to correct false impressions.

120

People v. Sala, 95 N.Y.2d 254, 739 N.E.2d 727, 716 N.Y.S.2d 361 (2000)

As former principals of First Meridian Planning Corporation, defendants were convicted of various crimes arising out of a scheme to defraud investors. All defendants challenge the legal sufficiency of the evidence as to fraudulent intent—a necessary element in all of the crimes charged. Because this contention lacks merit, we affirm the order of the Appellate Division. Another aspect of this appeal requires us to consider our power to address an issue raised by two of the defendants: whether a conviction for grand larceny by false pretenses (Penal Law 155.05[2][a]) may be based merely upon the concealment or omission of material facts. For reasons that follow, we are unable to reach this question.

Defendants Roger V. Sala, John Donovan and Roger C. Sala were each indicted on one count of Scheme to Defraud in the first degree (Penal Law 190.65[1]). Roger V. and Donovan were also indicted on 16 counts of grand larceny (Penal Law 155.30; 155.35) and 16 counts of securities fraud (General Business Law 352-c[6]). Defendants were tried jointly.

While the indictment did not specify the theory on which the grand larceny counts rested, the People, in their bill of particulars and at trial, proceeded on the basis of a larceny by false pretenses. At the close of the People's case, Roger C. moved for a trial order of dismissal based on insufficiency of the evidence, upon which the court reserved decision. Defendants Roger V. and Donovan made similar motions. They identified specific alleged insufficiencies but did not assert—as they do now—that false pretenses larceny must rest on affirmative false statements and that omissions or concealments alone are insufficient. Supreme Court denied their motions and the case proceeded against all three as charged. Instructing the jury as to the "false statement" element of false pretenses larceny, the trial court stated that "[a] misstatement or representation is false, obviously, when it is untrue. Whether a statement or representation is false depends upon the facts as they existed at the time the statement or representation was made and not the facts as they may appear now with the benefit of hindsight."

The court, however, went on to state that "a representation or statement may be false when it constitutes a half truth or effectively conceals or omits a material fact." Sala and Donovan did not object to this formulation. The jury found all three defendants guilty on all counts. Prior to sentencing, the trial court dismissed the case against Roger C. The court then granted "reargument" on Roger V. and Donovan's dismissal motions and, on its own initiative, dismissed 10 of the 16 larceny counts against each of them. It ruled that larceny by false pretenses requires affirmative, overt misrepresentations, and that the proof revealed only defendants' "omissions with respect to the disclosure of fees and commissions and other matters."

The People appealed; Roger V. and Donovan cross-appealed. The Appellate Division modified the judgment, reinstating the jury verdicts on the dismissed counts and affirming defendants' convictions on the remaining counts. A Judge of this Court granted defendants leave to appeal. We now affirm.

At trial, the prosecution presented proof that defendants disguised First Meridian as an objective financial planning institution that employed expert advisers who developed individualized investment strategies for its investors. There was evidence that, in reality, defendants used First Meridian to channel investors' assets into the same three risky investment vehicles, while misrepresenting the risks involved and concealing the fact that the company earned substantial commissions on the investments. Indeed, the proof revealed that 85 percent of First Meridian's annual revenue was derived from these undisclosed commissions. Investors had no idea of this; defendants went to some length to keep them in the dark. We agree with the Appellate Division that the evidence at trial was legally sufficient to demonstrate defendants' fraudulent intent in relation to all counts.

In addition, Roger V. and Donovan argue that the evidence was insufficient to support their convictions on the larceny counts dismissed by the trial court, because an omission of material fact does not constitute a "false statement" for purposes of larceny by false pretenses. That argument, however, is not properly before this Court. The trial court instructed the jury that the definition of a "false statement" included both affirmative misrepresentations and any representation that "effectively conceals or omits a material fact." Defendants did not object to this construction. Given the jury's guilty verdict, our review is limited to whether there was legally sufficient evidence as to false statements based on the court's charge as given without exception. There was; and we must therefore affirm. While the Appellate Division went further and addressed the question whether a false pretenses larceny conviction could ever rest merely on material omissions or concealments, our affirmance does not reach this issue and we express no opinion on this point. The evidence was legally sufficient under the unchallenged charge and provided a proper basis for the jury's verdict. Accordingly, the order of the Appellate Division should be affirmed.

MULTIPLE CHOICE QUESTIONS

1. What is the mental state element for the property crimes discussed in this chapter?
   - A. Intent.
   - B. Recklessness.
   - C. Negligence.
   - D. All the above, depending on the circumstances.

2. What element does a robbery have that a larceny does not?
   - A. Value of the property taken.
   - B. Force.
   - C. All the above.
   - D. None of the above.

3. In the Sala case, above, what issue(s) did the Court of Appeals not decide?
   - A. Whether false pretenses can be a larceny.
   - B. Whether the defendants should have been charged with embezzlement.
   - C. Whether the omission of a material fact constitutes a false statement.
   - D. All of the above.

4. Which of the situations would meet the "force" or "threatened force" element of robbery?
   - A. Taking a wallet from the victim's pants' pocket and causing a bruise to the victim.
   - B. Pushing the victim.
   - C. The defendant's sticking his finger in a coat pocket and pretending to have a gun.
   - D. All the above.

5. Which of the following is not an element of a larceny?
   - A. Forcibly.
   - B. Taking.
   - C. Property.
   - D. With the intent to deprive permanently.

DISCUSSION QUESTIONS

1. Discuss the public policies behind the creation of property crimes. Would those crimes exist in a socialist country?

2. A customer goes to a grocery store to buy $2.00 worth of food. The customer gives the cashier a $5 bill to pay for the $2.00 worth of food. Thinking that the customer gave her a $10 bill, the cashier gives the customer $8 in change. If the customer realizes immediately that she has received too much money back and leaves the store, has the customer committed any crime?

3. Could a defendant be guilty of both larceny and robbery based on the same act? Why or why not?

4. Could a defendant be guilty of both embezzlement and extortion based on the same act? Why or why not?

5. In New York, how are the various degrees of larceny distinguished?

Chapter 12

Crimes against Public Order and Morals

Introduction

Because the legislature as the representative of the people has made certain conduct a crime, there is a sense in which every crime is one "against public order or morals." Indeed, in a formalistic or literal sense, a crime is a crime only because the legislature says it is. Moreover, depending on the culture, society, nation, or even state, criminal offenses can vary widely. For example, the Netherlands permits the possession and sale of drugs that would be strictly illegal everywhere in the United States. Other countries view some sexual offenses in the United States as reflective of a prudish and unenlightened society. However, Nevada permits and regulates prostitution. Even within the United States, states such as Nevada and New Jersey permit certain types of gambling, which would be treated as a felony in virtually every other state. Until February 1, 2001, a New York statute prohibited unmarried persons from engaging in most sexual activity other than sexual intercourse (Penal Law 130.38), although the statute was virtually never enforced.

New York's Approach to Public Order and Morals

All societies have almost always punished such *mala in se* crimes as murder, rape, and robbery. Other *mala in se* type crimes, such as assault, kidnapping, burglary, arson, and larceny, as discussed in the previous chapters, receive widespread condemnation. Aside from such crimes that directly harm persons and property or result in the loss of one's property, there is a group of crimes that are prohibited because they affect public sensibilities and the "quality of life," although these crimes too can have direct effects on persons and property. In New York, some of the crimes within this group include gambling (Penal Law article 225), prostitution (Penal Law article 230), and obscenity (Penal Law article 235).

Some commentators argue that such behaviors affect only consenting adults and should therefore not be criminalized. In response, states argue that gambling promotes organized crime, prostitution results in the wider spread of sexually transmitted diseases, and obscenity causes the exploitation of persons, sometimes including children, who perform sexual acts for widespread dissemination. Of course, those who favor gambling, prostitution, and obscenity would argue that the government should simply permit and regulate these matters so as to better regulate sexually transmitted diseases and the influence of organized crime. States have been less able to provide tangible arguments for their prohibitions on obscenity—sexually explicit expression portraying adult actors or models (see Miller v. California, 413 U.S. 15, 93 S.Ct. 2607, 37 L.Ed.2d 419 (1973)).

In the case of People v. Stein, below, the defendants were prosecuted for setting up a gambling pool to bet on horse races. Note in the opinion that the gambling would have been legal if the defendants had done their gambling through a New York State authorized racetrack. Consider whether it makes sense for society to punish the defendants criminally for conduct that would not be criminal if the defendants had used State facilities and clerks instead of engaging in private transactions.

People v. Stein, 112 N.Y.S.2d 291, 279 A.D. 1048 (1st Department 1952)

Twenty-one individuals invested money with defendants and became shareholders in a pool ... Defendant Walter Stein believed that he had devised a handicapping system, which, if used as a basis for daily bets on horse races, would procure sure winnings for the participants. Of the persons intrigued by defendants' get rich quick system, some were close relatives, others were clients of defendant Walter Stein's accounting firm, and still others were neighbors or friends. Wagers were made from day to day by the three defendants on a large number of horses running in separate races at various tracks about the country. After the results of the bets were determined, the account of each one of the participants was credited with its share of the winnings or losses. On the losing bets the defendants received a commission from each of the book-makers with whom they did business of 3% or 4%. Defendants testified that these commissions were credited to an account which ultimately was to be used for the benefit of the participants in the pool. Through the instrumentality of wire tapping, police officers overheard large bets being placed with book-makers over the telephone in the offices used by defendants for the conduct of their profession of accounting. The question presented is whether under that set of facts defendants are merely players, as they claim, or whether their conduct constitutes a violation of ...the Penal Law.

In this case there was no proof that defendants were making a business of accepting bets from others in the organized business of book-making. However, the evidence concededly established that defendants placed with book-makers large bets daily on the outcome of horse races on behalf of themselves and on behalf of others, and that on the losing bets they derived from the book-makers a commission of 3% or 4%. The law forbids wagering and betting... except where the wagering is done at a duly authorized pari-mutuel race track in accordance with chapter 254 of the Laws of 1940, McK. Unconsol.Laws, § 7561 et seq. It is well settled that a bettor or player, as such, cannot be subjected to criminal prosecution under the law. A mere player is guilty of no crime...[T]he Penal Law does not apply 'to those who place their own bets with bookmakers, but to the professional operator who makes a business of betting against the public's guesses'. People v. Goldstein, 295 N.Y. 61, 63, 65 N.E.2d 169, 170. Where a person places bets with book-makers for himself *and for others* he violates ...the Penal Law....

Here defendants placed bets with book-makers on behalf of themselves and others. They were systematically forwarding bets on behalf of others and acting as custodians of money to be used for gambling purposes contrary to law. Indeed, the Court of Appeals in effect has held such acts unlawful ....

Defendants here were found guilty of five separate counts charging the crime of book-making on November 6, 1950. On each of these counts the court imposed upon defendants Walter Stein and Herman Stein a sentence of a fine of $500 or thirty days' imprisonment, plus six months in the city prison, execution of which was suspended; and upon defendant Israel a suspended sentence of six months in the workhouse.

We are of the view that the judgment of conviction as to count 'two' of the information which charges the defendants with receiving, registering and recording money bet upon the results of horse races, and as to count 'six' of the information charging the crime of conspiracy was adequately sustained by the evidence and should be affirmed. The judgment as to counts 'one', 'three', 'four' and 'five' of the information should be reversed, and as to each of such counts the information should be dismissed and the fines remitted.

No one of these defendants was engaged in book-making as a profession. The case is a border line one. In the circumstances, we think that the sentences were excessive, and that imposition of a jail sentence was not warranted. As to defendants Walter Stein and Herman Stein the sentence on the second count of the information should be modified by eliminating that portion of the sentence which directed that defendants serve six months in the workhouse, and the sentence on the sixth count should be modified by eliminating the prison sentence and to provide instead a fine of $500 or thirty days in the city prison. As to defendant Israel, sentence on the two counts should be suspended.

Judgment unanimously modified in accordance with the opinion herein. Settle order on notice. All concur.

The next case, People v Pinkoski, illustrates how the New York courts have interpreted New York's obscenity statutes. Note how the court in this case reacts to the judgment of the jury as to the appropriate community standard. Note also that the court is concerned about criminalizing conduct that may be innocent or that may have artistic value.

People v. Pinkoski, 752 N.Y.S.2d 421, 300 A.D.2d 834 (3rd Department 2002)

In September 2000, defendant took photographs of her six-year-old daughter (hereinafter the victim) posing in various stages of undress, while her five- year-old son and seven-year-old daughter were present. As relevant here, the photographs depict the victim lying on a bed with her raised buttocks exposed, squatting cross-legged on the floor with her bare buttocks exposed, standing with her shorts pulled down and her genitals exposed, pulling her shirt up with her bare chest exposed, and squatting with her buttocks exposed as an adult's hands spread her buttocks apart. These photographs and their negatives were the basis of a 19-count indictment handed down in March 2001. The indictment charges defendant with five counts of using a child in a sexual performance (see

Penal Law 263.05), five counts of promoting a sexual performance by a child (see Penal Law 263.15), five counts of possession of a sexual performance by a child (see Penal Law 263.16), one count of sexual abuse in the first degree (see Penal Law 130.65[3]) and three counts of endangering the welfare of a child (see Penal Law 260.10).

Both testimonial and documentary evidence was presented to the grand jury. An employee of the Wal-Mart Photo Center testified that during his development of the film, he discovered the photographs of a partially clad young girl "posing for the camera." He reported the photographs to the store manager who promptly called the police. The police confiscated only the subject photographs; the remaining photographs and all the negatives were returned.

William Carpenter, a detective with the City of Cortland Police Department in Cortland County, testified that he met defendant at the children's elementary school.... When first confronted with these photographs, defendant expressed disgust and shock, denying any involvement. However, after a further interview, she provided a written statement in which she admitted that she took the photographs, but explained that the activity was unplanned--she had a camera in her hand when the victim jokingly suggested, "do you want to see my butt." While laughing, the victim laid on defendant's bed and then pulled down her shorts and underwear exposing her buttocks; defendant took a photograph. The victim then got up off the bed and squatted on the floor cross-legged while still partially clothed; defendant took a photograph. Once dressed, the victim inquired about the differences between boys and girls as discussed in her school sex education program ... and then pulled down her shorts and underwear; defendant "accidentally took a photograph of [the victim's] vagina." With the victim thereafter "ask[ing] * * * about her butt," defendant again took a photograph, not realizing that the camera was on, when the victim pulled her butt cheeks apart with her hands. Concluding by pulling up her shorts, the victim then lifted up the front of her shirt showing her bare chest; defendant took another photograph. In her statement, defendant admitted to knowing that both her five-year-old son and seven-year-old daughter were present in the bedroom while the photographs were taken and, watching from the hallway, was her boyfriend, Henry Randall. Clearly aware of her inappropriate conduct, she admitted, "I know that I should not have taken photographs of [the victim] with her shorts pulled down exposing herself," and conceded, "I also probably should not have taken photographs while my other children were in the bedroom watching."

After the police interviewed Randall, defendant's interview continued and her statement further evolved, now disclosing that she had not been entirely truthful. Pertaining to the photograph separating the victim's buttocks, defendant explained that she "gave [her other] daughter the camera as [she] pulled [the victim's] butt cheeks apart to see if [she] had any bruises on her. As [she] was pulling [her] butt cheeks apart * * * [her other daughter] took a picture of [her] doing this * * *." Defendant then offered a new explanation for her conduct: "The reason I had [the victim] show her vagina and her butt to me was because I was trying to teach [her] about sex education. On this date I was trying to teach my kids what is right about sex and what is wrong about sex." Randall's testimony before the grand jury recounted how he accidentally stumbled upon this incident, expressing "shock" at defendant's behavior. He confirmed that the victim was not fully clothed when photographed and that defendant was the one who held the victim's "butt cheeks" apart.

At the conclusion of all testimony, the grand jury was provided with a description of the charges, the elements of the crimes, definitions of all relevant terms as set forth in Penal Law 263.00, and the available affirmative defense. It was instructed on the applicable standard of proof and told to consider all 19 counts. After voting to return the full indictment, County Court granted defendant's motion to dismiss. The People appeal.

In assessing the proffer made to the grand jury, we view the evidence in the light most favorable to the People to determine whether this evidence "'if unexplained and uncontradicted would warrant conviction by a petit jury'" (People v. Jensen, 86 N.Y.2d 248, 251, 630 N.Y.S.2d 989, 654 N.E.2d 1237). As long as the grand jury could have rationally drawn the inference of guilt, we must find the evidence legally sufficient.

Addressing the dismissal of those counts predicated upon photographs of the victim's buttocks and bare chest as not constituting a "lewd exhibition of the genitals" within the meaning of sexual conduct as defined in Penal Law 263.00(3), we can find no error. Generally, we will not supply, by implication, a provision in a statute when it is reasonable to believe that its absence was intended by the Legislature.... With a penal statute, it is further presumed that its terms are to "be construed according * * * [their] fair import * * * to promote justice and effect the objects of the law" (Penal Law 5.00). Hence, where, as here, the Legislature has chosen to define the term "sexual conduct" four different ways in four separate sections of the Penal Law and, in only two such sections is the term "buttocks" specifically included, the absence of such language in Penal Law 263.00 is dispositive. Yielding to the cautionary language from the U.S. Supreme Court that "[t]he category of 'sexual conduct' proscribed must * * * be suitably limited and described" (New York v. Ferber, 458 U.S. 747, 764), we can find no basis upon which to supplement, by implication, the controlling provisions of this statute. For all of these reasons, we must affirm the dismissal of those counts.

We are of a different view with regard to County Court's dismissal of those counts of the indictment premised upon the photograph of the victim's genitalia, due to the insufficiency of the grand jury instructions. While it might have been preferable for the People to have instructed the grand jury as to the generally accepted definitions of the term "lewd," the word is not so arcane as to escape the understanding of the average juror. Lewd has been defined as "characterized by lust, obscene or indecent" (The Random House Dictionary of the English Language 825 [unabridged ed 1966]), "showing or intended to excite lust or sexual desire, esp. in an offensive way" (Webster's New World College Dictionary 825 [4th ed 1999]) and " offensive to accepted standards of decency" (Roget's II The New Thesaurus 658 [1986]). The photograph in question depicts a frontal view of the victim with her pants down to her ankles and with her left hand on her stomach and her right hand on her groin area in close proximity to her genitalia, as if she were about to fondle herself or entice the viewer to do so. Such depiction is far from that of a family photograph of a nude child either lying on a blanket or bathing, and assuredly could not be considered an artistic rendering of a nude. To the contrary, a grand jury could well conclude, as it did here, that the photograph was sexual in nature, offensive to accepted standards of decency and intended to appeal to the prurient interests of the pedophile viewer.

We also find that the charge of sexual abuse in the first degree, grounded upon defendant's spreading of the child's buttocks, must be reinstated. In light of defendant's inconsistent and disingenuous statements explaining the basis for the photographs, the grand jury could properly infer the sexual gratification element from her conduct … Finally addressing the remaining counts of the indictment alleging that defendant's conduct endangered the welfare of her children, her admissions conceding the inappropriate nature of her conduct wholly supports the grand jury's conclusion that she was aware that her conduct was harmful.

Ordered that the order is modified, on the law, by reversing so much thereof as granted defendant's motion to dismiss counts 3, 8, 13, 16, 17, 18 and 19 of the indictment; motion denied to that extent and said counts reinstated; and, as so modified, affirmed.

In New York, there is another group of crimes that are deemed to be "offenses against public order, public sensibilities and the right to privacy" (Title N of the Penal Law). This group includes offenses contained in article 240 (offenses against public order), article 241 (harassment of rent regulated tenants), article 245 (offenses against public sensibilities), and Article 250 (offenses against the right to privacy) of the Penal Law. In addition, in Title O, Article 255, the Penal Law regulates conduct affecting the "marital relationship."

While the creation in the Penal Law of most offenses against public order (such as inciting to riot, aggravated harassment, and falsely reporting an emergency) would seem to have widespread support, the creation of some crimes can be more controversial. For example, the Penal Law prohibits "loitering," which includes begging and sleeping in a transportation facility (240.35 (1) & (7)), although loitering is classified as a "violation," not a crime. Despite its status as a violation, however, loitering is punishable by up to 15 days imprisonment (70.15(4)). Advocates of homeless persons would argue that "loitering" is the activity in which some persons in society must engage to survive.

Examine the Bright case, in which the defendant is arrested for "loitering" in a transportation facility, and determine whether it would be possible to draft a statute, other than loitering, to eliminate the "quality of life" problems at issue in the Bright case, such as sleeping in a train station. In a train station, for example, consider how the State might limit the station's use to people who are using the trains or the facilities. Presumably, the legislature could write a law that said, "Only persons who are riding the trains within one hour or who have ridden the trains within the past hour can be inside the train station." Such a law is precise and clear. The only way police officers can determine whether someone is "using" the train station, however, is to ask the person. In the Bright case, the court holds that a "suspect" who is asked his business in the train station cannot be made to answer because such compulsion would violate his right to remain silent.

People v. Bright, 71 N.Y.2d 376, 520 N.E.2d 1355, 526 N.Y.S.2d 66 (1988)

[This case involves two defendants, one named Bright and the other named Clark. They were both arrested in New York pursuant to a loitering statute, and both appealed their convictions to the New York Court of Appeals.]

The issue presented on these two appeals is whether Penal Law 240.35(7), which provides that "[a] person is guilty of loitering when he * * * [loiters] or remains in any transportation facility, or is found sleeping therein, and is unable to give a satisfactory explanation of his presence," is constitutional. We hold that this statute is unconstitutionally vague under the Due Process Clauses of the Federal and State Constitutions because it fails to give fair notice to the ordinary citizen that the prohibited conduct is illegal, it lacks minimal legislative guidelines, thereby permitting arbitrary enforcement and, finally, it requires that a citizen relinquish his constitutional right against compulsory self-incrimination in order to avoid arrest.

People v Bright

On the evening of March 19, 1985, a New York City policeman observed defendant Bright displaying an open satchel to a passerby on the Long Island Railroad Concourse located in Pennsylvania Station. When Bright noticed that the officer was watching him, he quickly closed the satchel. The policeman approached Bright and the following conversation took place:

> Officer: What are you doing here?
> Defendant: Why are you bothering me?
> Officer: Got a ticket to take the train?
> Defendant: No.
> Officer: Any money to buy a ticket?
> Defendant: No.
> Officer: Are you going to take the train?
> Defendant: No.

Based solely on this exchange, the officer escorted Bright to the Long Island Railraod police office, where he asked Bright to produce identification. When Bright failed to produce any, the officer informed him that he was under arrest for loitering pursuant to Penal Law 240.35(7). Bright was read his Miranda warnings and asked to empty his pockets. As Bright removed a piece of paper from his trouser pocket, two credit cards and four other identification cards fell to the floor, none of which belonged to him. Bright then told the officer that he had found the various cards and planned to sell them.

Defendant Bright was charged by indictment with two counts of criminal possession of stolen property in the second degree (Penal Law 165.45[2]), and one count of criminal possession of stolen property in the third degree (Penal Law 165.40). On his pretrial motion to suppress the physical evidence, Bright argued that he was arrested without probable cause, and that his arrest was illegal, since the loitering statute pursuant to which he was arrested was unconstitutional. The Supreme Court … held that the statute was unconstitutionally vague and granted the suppression motion on the theory that the arrest was violative of the defendant's constitutional rights. A unanimous Appellate Division affirmed, without opinion.

People v Clark

On the morning of April 24, 1985, defendant Clark was in the Port Authority Bus Terminal located in New York City when he was approached by a Port Authority police officer. Although the record is not entirely clear as to what occurred next, the officer arrested Clark for loitering in violation of Penal Law 240.35(7) when he was unable to give a satisfactory explanation regarding his presence in the bus terminal. As an incident to that arrest, the officer searched Clark and found a cellophane envelope containing cocaine and a glass pipe with cocaine residue in the defendant's jacket pocket.

Clark was charged with loitering (Penal Law 240.35[7]), and criminal possession of a controlled substance in the seventh degree (Penal Law 220.03). At his arraignment before the Criminal Court of the City of New York, Clark moved to dismiss the loitering charge on the ground that Penal Law 240.35(7) was unconstitutionally vague. His motion was denied, and he was permitted to plead guilty to a violation of the loitering statute in satisfaction of both charges. On appeal before the Appellate Term, First Department, the court held that the statute was unconstitutionally vague and reversed the conviction, dismissed the loitering charge and remanded the case to the Criminal Court for further proceedings on the charge of criminal possession of a controlled substance.

In each of these two cases, a Judge of this court granted the People leave to appeal so that we could consider the constitutionality of Penal Law 240.35(7). We have examined the People's arguments in support of the statute, but agree with the defendants that the statute is void for vagueness, and we now affirm in both cases.

The legislative history … indicates that the subways and railroad stations had become an attractive place for "fakers, perverts, pickpockets, loiterers, sleepers, flimflam men, etc., [who] [infested] these properties, night and day, necessitating constant policing by a large force of special officers and state railway officers" (Bill Jacket, L 1939, ch 391, Senate Mem, at 4). Public officials and railroad authorities sought to prevent "peddlers and loiterers from harassing and annoying people on the railroad properties." The Legislature, aware that the courts were refusing to convict people arrested in the train and subway stations of vagrancy or disorderly conduct, considered the bill necessary to protect the traveling public, especially because of the desire to "clean up" the subways and other railroad facilities in anticipation of the World's Fair held in New York City in 1939.

In a challenge to the constitutionality of a penal law on the grounds of vagueness, it is well settled that a two-pronged analysis is required. First, the statute must provide sufficient notice of what conduct is prohibited; second, the statute must not be written in such a manner as to permit or encourage arbitrary and discriminatory enforcement. The rationale underlying the requirement that a penal statute provide adequate notice is the notion "that no man shall be held criminally responsible for conduct which he could not reasonably understand to be proscribed." Consistent with our concept of basic fairness, due process requires that a penal statute be sufficiently definite by its terms so as "to give a person of ordinary intelligence fair notice that his contemplated conduct is forbidden by the statute." For this reason, under our State and Federal Constitutions, the Legislature may not criminalize conduct that is inherently innocent merely because such conduct is "sometimes attended by improper motives," since to do so would not fairly inform the ordinary citizen that an otherwise innocent act is illegal.

The other prong of the test, which requires that a penal law not permit arbitrary or discriminatory enforcement is, perhaps, the more important aspect of the vagueness doctrine. The Legislature must include in a penal statute "minimal guidelines to govern law enforcement." The absence of objective standards to guide those enforcing the laws permits the police to make arrests based upon their own personal, subjective idea of right and wrong. A vague statute "confers on police a virtually unrestrained power to arrest and charge persons with a violation."

The thrust of the People's argument on this appeal in support of the statute is twofold. First, the People argue that the "satisfactory explanation" provision in the statute is constitutionally permissible. Second, the People take the position that Penal Law 240.35(7) falls within the category of statutes prohibiting loitering in specific places of restricted public access.

Regardless of whether one characterizes the "satisfactory explanation" requirement as substantive or procedural, in People v Berck, we concluded that a similar provision in a loitering statute that required a person to "identify himself" or "give a reasonably credible account of his conduct and purposes" was unconstitutional. We held that under this provision, "enforcement of the law depends entirely upon whether the arresting officer is satisfied that a suspect has given" an acceptable account of his presence.

Requiring a person suspected of violating the loitering statute provide a "satisfactory explanation" to avoid arrest is also violative of a citizen's right not to answer questions posed by law enforcement officers. Although a police officer may have the right under appropriate circumstances to stop a person in a public place and make inquiry (see Terry v Ohio, 392 U.S. 1), a citizen is under no obligation to provide any explanation regarding his conduct.

Moreover, the statute is unconstitutionally vague, since it provides absolutely no legislative "guidelines governing the determination as to whether a person is engaged in suspicious loitering" in places of unrestricted public. In such large, urban transportation facilities, many people are engaged in activity that is seemingly aimless to the objective observer, such as waiting for a train, strolling about the concourse, or waiting for the rain to stop. Nevertheless, who will be stopped, questioned, and arrested under this statute is left "solely up to the discretion of the police officer" on the scene. Inasmuch as we have concluded that Penal Law 240.35(7) is unconstitutional, we need not reach defendant Bright's claim that the police lacked probable cause to arrest him. Accordingly, the orders appealed from in both cases should be affirmed.

Arbitrariness

In the Bright case, the court was concerned that the police could misuse a very broad loitering statute by applying it to virtually anyone, including, for example, someone a police officer simply disliked. Such broad statutes can result in arbitrary or preferential law enforcement. Arbitrariness can also result, however, when a statute specifically indicates the intended class of defendants who will be covered by the statute. Moreover, it can be the legislature rather than the police that creates the arbitrariness.

For example, the Penal Law contains a statute titled, "Appearance in public under the influence of narcotics or a drug other than alcohol" (Penal Law 240.40). Under this statute, it is a violation to appear "in public under the influence of narcotics or a drug other than alcohol." The statute is presumably designed to prevent rude, ill-mannered, and obnoxious behavior in public. Such a statute punishes those who are "obnoxious" in public as a result of using some type of drug, either an illegal drug or a legal prescription drug. Ironically, appearing to be under the influence of (or being obnoxious because of) alcohol, which is itself a drug, is not prohibited by the statute.

If the legislature's goal is to protect public sensibilities by prohibiting obnoxiousness in pubic (such as the appearance of being "under the influence"), then it makes no difference whether someone's obnoxiousness is caused by alcohol or marijuana or codeine. It would seem rational to prohibit all people from appearing in public when they are under the influence of a substance or drug, regardless of what is the substance or drug. It is true that the legislature might argue that the passage of such a statute (appearing under the influence in public) limits police authority, because most of the people who appear intoxicated in public will have come to their state of intoxication through the use of alcohol, and they will never be arrested. That argument, however, might result in law enforcement arbitrariness toward persons under the influence of any legal or illegal drug other than alcohol, and preferences for those under the influence of the drug alcohol.

A legislative decision that society should protect the alcohol abuser but not the marijuana or codeine abuser seems highly arbitrary. The public obnoxiousness of each might be exactly the same. It would seem fair that drug abusers, regardless of the drug they abuse, should be treated similarly—either they should all be punished for their public behavior as a means to deter them from abusing drugs or irritating other citizens, or they should all be treated for their drug abuse, or they should all be left alone.

These examples illustrate how some crimes against "public sensibilities" can be controversial because they seem only to affect a dispossessed subset of persons (such as impoverished beggars or homeless persons). Similarly, some crimes reflect societal confusion or hypocrisy by punishing only arbitrarily selected persons, such as those who abuse any drug other than alcohol. It does not seem to make sense to prohibit only a small subset of—persons—those who ingest drugs other than alcohol, for example—from appearing intoxicated in public, unless, of course, there are factors present in the formulation of law other than the quest for blind justice. Perhaps, in passing the law that prohibits "appearing under the influence of a drug other than alcohol in public," the legislature believed that it could overcome the objections of marijuana growers to the law but not those of the alcohol industry.

Nonetheless, many professionals are involved in the quest for justice. Police officers can use their discretion not to arrest, and prosecutors can use their discretion not to prosecute. Judges might find unconstitutional on equal protection grounds the statute that favors alcohol users over other drug users. Juries are always the final barrier between the people and the government. Whatever one's place in the justice system, the goal is to apply laws fairly and achieve justice, a quest that will continue through all ages.

MULTIPLE CHOICE QUESTIONS

1. In the Bright case, the statute was unconstitutional because it was:
   A. Precise.
   B. Vague.
   C. Violated equal protection.
   D. Cruel and inhuman.

2. What would be an example of a "public order" violation?
   A. Larceny.
   B. Appearing intoxicated in public.
   C. Drug sales.
   D. All the above.

3. Which of the following are criminal offenses in New York?
   A. Appearing intoxicated in public.
   B. Loitering in public.
   C. Robbery.
   D. All the above.

4. Vague laws can lead to police:
   A. Burnout.
   B. Arbitrariness.
   C. Dissatisfaction.
   D. All the above.

5. New York has criminal laws against:
   A. Sexually transmitted diseases.
   B. Obscenity.
   C. Pornography.
   D. All the above.

DISCUSSION EXERCISES

1. Why was the statute in the Bright case held unconstitutional?

2. Given the decision in the Bright case, what can New York do to ensure that people do not use the train stations as homes?

3. If you could, what criminal statutes, if any, would you eliminate, and why?

4. How much influence does the free market economic system have on the formulation of laws?

5. Discuss whether any of the crimes noted in this chapter are "victimless" crimes. If a crime is a victimless crime, could there still be a reason for retaining it?

6. What criminal statutes could be added to the Penal Law to address conduct that causes problems for society?

Chapter 13

Crimes against the State

The expression, "crimes against the state," has traditionally referred to crimes that affect national security, such as treason and espionage. Treason and espionage relate to actions that a person takes to aid other countries in undermining the United States government. New York has no statutes relating to treason or espionage. New York does have Penal Law statutes related to "Terrorism." The legislature passed the statutes following the World Trade Center attacks of September 11, 2001. However, the State of New York has brought no prosecutions under these statutes, mainly because the federal government takes responsibility for handling the prevention and prosecution of terrorism and "crimes against the state."

Thus, federal constitutional and statutory law will provide the basis for almost all prosecutions of persons facing charges related to the overthrow of the national government. Although a person might commit actions to undermine the state government in Albany, New York State criminal law probably would be sufficient to prosecute such a person. Moreover, state criminal law is usually sufficient to prosecute persons who the state or federal governments label as "terrorists."

For example, one of the alleged Oklahoma City bombers, Terry Nichols, was convicted under federal law for his part in the bombing of the federal building in 1995 in Oklahoma City, where the blast killed 168 people. Perhaps one might think of the bombing as a "crime against the state" because the bombers were reportedly motivated by anti-government feelings. The state of Oklahoma was dissatisfied with Nichols' federal sentence, which did not include the death penalty. In response, Oklahoma tried Nichols for murder, a basic criminal offense in every state.

Of course, since the early 1990s, terrorists have focused on New York City. Their acts have included the World Trade Center airplane attacks of September 11, 2001 and the first World Trade Center bombing in 1993. The 1993 bombers were prosecuted and convicted under federal law. In flying the planes into the World Trade Center towers, the 2001 bombers committed suicide. New York State could have prosecuted any of the bombers for murder and arson related offenses, among many other crimes.

Following the World Trade Center bombings of 2001, New York passed Article 490 of the Penal Law, which is entitled, "Terrorism." This Article includes six crimes with titles that relate to terrorism. The crimes include soliciting terrorism in the first and second degrees, hindering prosecution of terrorism in the first and second degrees, making a terroristic threat, and terrorism (Penal Law 490.10-490.35).

The crimes in Article 490 ("Terrorism") are relatively unique because they contain an element of "motivation," an element absent from most criminal statutes. The element of motivation comes from the "Crime of terrorism," which is contained in Penal Law 490.25.

The motivation element relates to an attempt to influence the government through harming the civilian population.

More specifically, the crime of terrorism is defined as an intentional act designed to "intimidate or coerce a civilian population, influence the policy of a unit of government by intimidation or coercion, or affect the conduct of a unit of government by murder, assassination or kidnapping" (Penal Law 490.25(1). The intentional acts required as part of a terrorism offense are termed "specified offenses." Specified offenses include Class A felonies, such as murder, among other offenses.

Absent the element of motivation (that is, committing a specified crime to intimidate a civilian population or to influence the government), the crimes that a terrorist commits could routinely be prosecuted under traditional Penal Law statutes. Nonetheless, the main import of Article 490 (related to terrorism) is to increase the severity of sentences for defendants convicted of traditional criminal offenses, when those defendants possessed a motivation to intimidate a civilian population or influence the government through illegal activity. For example, for sentencing purposes, a felony will be increased one class if the felony was a specified crime under Penal Law 490.05(3) (that is, a crime related to terrorism, as defined in the Penal Law). The punishment for class C, D, and E felonies will be increased one class, and B felonies will be increased to a class A-I felony.

The Ramzi Yousef case, below, outlines the origins of the terrorist threat to New York City. The Yousef case involves a federal prosecution. In reading the case, note the charges that the federal government brought against the defendants. Consider whether the federal government is the most appropriate entity to prosecute terrorist conspiracies. Also, consider whether suspects apprehended outside the territory of the United States should be afforded all the protections of the United States Constitution.

United States v. Yousef, 327 F.3d 56 (2003)

Defendants-appellants Ramzi Yousef, Eyad Ismoil, and Abdul Hakim Murad appeal from judgments of conviction entered in the United States District Court for the Southern District of New York on April 13, June 2, and June 15, 1998, respectively. Judge Duffy presided over two separate jury trials. In the first trial, Yousef, Murad, and Wali Khan Amin Shah were tried on charges relating to a conspiracy to bomb United States commercial airliners in Southeast Asia. In the second trial, Yousef and Ismoil were tried for their involvement in the February 1993 bombing of the World Trade Center in New York City. Yousef, Ismoil, and Murad now appeal from their convictions, asserting a number of claims.

The conspiracy to bomb the World Trade Center began in the Spring of 1992, when Yousef met Ahmad Mohammad Ajaj at a terrorist training camp on the border of Afghanistan and Pakistan. After formulating their terrorist plot, Yousef and Ajaj traveled to New York together in September 1992. In Ajaj's luggage, he carried a "terrorist kit" that included, among other things, bomb-making manuals. After Yousef and Ajaj arrived at John F. Kennedy International Airport, inspectors of the Immigration and Naturalization Service ("INS") discovered the "terrorist kit" in Ajaj's luggage and arrested him. Although Yousef was also stopped, he and Ajaj did not disclose their connection to one another, and INS officials allowed Yousef to enter the United States.

Once in New York, Yousef began to put together the manpower and the supplies that he would need to carry out his plan to bomb the World Trade Center. Yousef assembled a group of co-conspirators to execute his plan, including defendants Mohammad Salameh, Nidal Ayyad, Mahmud Abouhalima, and Abdul Rahman Yasin. Next, Yousef began accumulating the necessary ingredients for the bomb. He ordered the required chemicals, and his associates rented a shed in which to store them. Yousef and Salameh established their headquarters at an apartment they rented in Jersey City, New Jersey, an urban center located across the Hudson River from Manhattan. The apartment also functioned as their bomb-making factory.

In December 1992, Yousef contacted Ismoil, who was then living in Dallas, Texas.... On February 22, 1993, Ismoil joined Yousef and the others in New York to help complete the bomb preparations.

On February 26, 1993, Yousef and Ismoil drove a bomb-laden van onto the B-2 level of the parking garage below the World Trade Center. They then set the bomb's timer to detonate minutes later. At approximately 12:18 p.m. that day, the bomb exploded, killing six people, injuring more than a thousand others and causing widespread fear and more than $500 million in property damage.

Soon after the bombing, Yousef and Ismoil fled from the United States. Yousef and Ismoil were indicted for their participation in the bombing on March 31, 1993 and August 8, 1994, respectively. Yousef was captured in Pakistan nearly two years after the bombing, and Ismoil was arrested in Jordan a little over two years after the attack. Both were returned to the United States to answer the charges in the indictment....

Airline Bombing

A year and a half after the World Trade Center bombing, Yousef entered Manila, the capital of the Philippines, under an assumed name. By September 1994, Yousef had devised a plan to attack United States airliners. According to the plan, five individuals would place bombs aboard twelve United States-flag aircraft that served routes in Southeast Asia. The conspirators would board an airliner in Southeast Asia, assemble a bomb on the plane, and then exit the plane during its first layover. As the planes continued on toward their next destinations, the time-bombs would detonate. Eleven of the twelve flights targeted were ultimately destined for cities in the United States....

Yousef and his co-conspirators performed several tests in preparation for the airline bombings. In December 1994, Yousef and Wali Khan Amin Shah placed one of the bombs they had constructed in a Manila movie theater. The bomb exploded, injuring several patrons of the theater. Ten days later, Yousef planted another test bomb under a passenger's seat during the first leg of a Philippine Airlines flight from Manila to Japan. Yousef disembarked from the plane during the stopover and then made his way back to Manila. During the second leg of the flight, the bomb exploded, killing one passenger, a Japanese national, and injuring others.

The plot to bomb the United States-flag airliners was uncovered in January 1995, only two weeks before the conspirators intended to carry it out. Yousef and Murad were burning chemicals in their Manila apartment and accidentally caused a fire. An apartment security guard saw the smoke coming from the apartment and called the fire department. After the firemen left, the Philippine police arrived at the apartment, where they discovered chemicals and bomb components, a laptop computer on which Yousef had set forth the aircraft bombing plans, and other incriminating evidence. Philippine authorities arrested Murad and Shah, though Shah escaped and was not recaptured until nearly a year later. Yousef fled the country, but was captured in Pakistan the next month....

On February 21, 1996, a grand jury in the Southern District of New York filed a twenty-count superseding indictment against the defendants and others. Counts One through Eleven charged Yousef and Ismoil with various offenses arising from their participation in the February 26, 1993 bombing of the World Trade Center. Counts Twelve through Nineteen charged Yousef, Murad, and Shah with various crimes relating to their conspiracy to bomb United States airliners in Southeast Asia in 1994 and 1995....

The trial of Yousef, Murad, and Shah on the airline bombing charges began on May 29, 1996 and ended on September 5, 1996, when the jury found all three defendants guilty on all counts. Yousef and Ismoil's trial on charges relating to the World Trade Center bombing began on July 15, 1997 and concluded on November 12, 1997, when the jury found both defendants guilty on all counts.

Yousef was sentenced for both convictions on January 8, 1998. For the World Trade Center convictions he was sentenced principally to a total of 240 years of imprisonment....

Preparation for Airline Bombing Conspiracy

In August 1994, after the bombing of the World Trade Center and his flight from the United States, Yousef traveled to Manila under an alias. By September, Yousef had developed an elaborate plan to bomb a dozen United States-flag aircraft and recorded that plan on his laptop computer. According to the plan, five individuals would plant bombs aboard twelve United States-flag aircraft operating on routes in Southeast Asia. Each conspirator would board an airliner in Southeast Asia, assemble a bomb on board the plane, and leave the aircraft at its first stop. The time-bombs would detonate during the second leg of each of the targeted flights. Eleven of the twelve flights were ultimately destined for cities in the United States. Each of the targeted aircraft was capable of carrying up to 280 people.

After Yousef had formulated his airline bombing plan, he began to acquire the information

141

and the ingredients necessary to carry it out. Yousef compiled detailed flight data on the twelve aircraft, including their departing times, flight numbers, flight durations and aircraft types, and transferred this information to his laptop computer. In early November 1994, Yousef placed a large order for chemicals and equipment in Manila, and, during the next two months, he and his co-conspirators performed several tests in preparation for the aircraft bombings. On December 1, 1994, Yousef and Shah conducted a test by placing a bomb under a patron's seat at the Greenbelt movie theater in Manila. At 10: 30 p.m., the bomb exploded, injuring several people. Ten days later, on December 11, Yousef planted another test bomb under the seat of a passenger on a Philippine Airlines jet flying from Manila to Cebu (another city in the Philippines) and then to Japan. Yousef disembarked from the plane in Cebu. Two hours after the aircraft departed from Cebu, the bomb exploded, killing one Japanese passenger and injuring others.

In late December, Murad traveled from the Middle East to the Philippines, and Shah, who had left the Philippines immediately after the movie theater bombing, returned to Manila under an assumed name. Thus, by January 1995, the conspirators were assembled in Manila and ready to carry out their attack on twelve United States-flag aircraft. But for a fire in the defendants' apartment in Manila, the plan might have succeeded....

Discovery of Airline Bombing Plot

On January 6, 1995, Yousef was in the Manila apartment burning chemicals that he and Murad had obtained to construct the aircraft bombs. At approximately 10:45 p.m., an apartment security guard noticed Yousef and Murad running down the stairs carrying their shoes. After Yousef and Murad went back to their apartment, their neighbors observed smoke coming from the window of their apartment and alerted apartment security. The security guard proceeded to the apartment to investigate, finding Murad and Yousef by their front door. The defendants denied that there was a fire in their apartment and would not permit the guard inside to inspect. The guard then returned to his post to contact the police.

After trying to contact the local police to no avail, the security guard returned to the apartment to investigate further. At this point, Murad let the security guard into the apartment, while Yousef waited outside. The guard observed a salt-like substance and burn marks in the area of the sink. Murad told the guard that they had been mixing ingredients to make firecrackers for a late New Year's celebration. The guard then went back to his station and had the receptionist call the fire department. In the meantime, Yousef left the apartment complex.

After the firefighters had come and gone, police arrived at the apartment. The security guard let the police into the apartment, where they found, among other things, cartons of chemicals, Casio timers, wrist watches with wires attached, and juice bottles with unknown substances inside. The officers then waited in the lobby of the apartment complex for Murad and Yousef to return. Murad returned and, after he was approached by one of the officers, tried to flee. The police quickly apprehended him and took him into custody.

While in custody at the apartment Murad called Yousef's cellular telephone. Almost immediately after receiving this call, Yousef made arrangements to leave the country. He purchased a plane ticket to Singapore and fled the Philippines approximately five hours after Murad's call.

While Yousef was in flight from the country, the police continued to search the Manila apartment. In addition to the … bomb-related materials, police discovered photographs of Pope John Paul II, Bibles, and confession materials; the Pope was scheduled to visit Manila on January 12, 1995, just five days later. The police collected some of the items they found in the apartment and then applied for a warrant to search the apartment. A Philippine judge issued a search warrant, and members of the local police explosive ordnance disposal unit ("EOD") conducted a thorough investigation of the apartment. They videotaped the contents of the apartment and seized several items, including Yousef's laptop computer, papers and books with instructions for making bombs, a chemical dictionary, and many chemicals and mechanical components which could have been used to make bombs. On Yousef's laptop computer the police found various files including a letter claiming responsibility for future attacks against American targets by the "Fifth Division of the Liberation Army"….

Arrests of Shah, Yousef, and Murad

On January 11, 1995, several days after their search of the Manila apartment, Manila police arrested Shah. Police apprehended Shah after they determined that a pager called by Yousef following Murad's arrest was registered in the name of Shah's girlfriend. Shah escaped from custody one week later, only to be recaptured on December 11, 1995 in Malaysia by Malaysian police. Shah was then delivered to the custody of the United States, where he agreed to speak to Federal Bureau of Investigation ("FBI") agents after he signed a written waiver of his *Miranda* rights.

In early February 1995, the United States Embassy in Islamabad, Pakistan received a tip that Yousef was somewhere in Islamabad. On February 7, 1995, Pakistani officials, together with a special agent from the United States Department of State, arrested Yousef at a guest house in Islamabad. The next day, agents from the FBI and the United States Secret Service arrived from the United States, took Yousef into custody, and transported him back to the United States. On the plane, Yousef was informed of the charges against him pertaining to the World Trade Center bombing and advised of his rights. Without the use or need of an interpreter, he waived his *Miranda* rights and made an extensive confession about the World Trade Center bombing plot.

Philippine authorities turned Murad over to FBI agents in Manila on April 12, 1995. During the plane ride to the United States, Murad was read his *Miranda* rights twice and given written copies of the waiver in both English and Arabic. Murad indicated that he understood his rights and waived them in writing. He then agreed to speak to the FBI agents on the airplane without an interpreter. Murad told the agents that his part in the aircraft bombing scheme was to board a United Airlines flight in Singapore with its first stop in Hong Kong and to plant a bomb onboard the plane. After arriving in Hong Kong, Murad was to take a different flight back to Singapore, planting a bomb aboard that plane as well. Murad told the agents that he expected the resulting explosion to tear a hole in the aircraft, causing it to crash in the Pacific Ocean. He also asserted his belief that co-conspirators would bomb other flights. Murad stated that the goal of the attacks was to "make the American people and the American government suffer for their support of Israel"....

Murad described the explosive device components of the bombs, which matched items seized at the Manila apartment he shared with Yousef. Murad stated that he had been told that the Philippine Airlines bombing of December 11, 1994 was a test-run to ensure that the chemicals and timing device worked correctly.

On February 21, 1996, a grand jury in the Southern District of New York indicted Yousef, Murad, and Shah for various crimes relating to their conspiracy to bomb United States airliners in Southeast Asia in 1994 and 1995. Counts Twelve through Twenty of the original indictment were renumbered from One to Nine for use in the airline bombing trial. In Count Twelve, the defendants were indicted for conspiring to [destroy] aircraft....

The judgments of the District Court are affirmed except to the extent that Ismoil's restitution requirements are hereby modified in the manner described above.

MULTIPLE CHOICE QUESTIONS

1. Espionage and treason are:
   A. Federal crimes.
   B. State crimes.
   C. Both A and B.
   D. Neither A nor B.

2. The unique element in the crime of Terrorism is:
   A. Actus reus.
   B. Mens rea.
   C. Causation.
   D. Motivation.

3. The Oklahoma City bombing resulted in:
   A. Federal prosecution.
   B. State prosecution.
   C. Both A and B.
   D. Neither A nor B.

4. Under Article 490, what would be a specified offense?
   A. Class A felony.
   B. Murder.
   C. Criminal tampering.
   D. All the above.

5. New York has criminal laws against:
   A. Terrorism.
   B. Soliciting terrorism.
   C. Hindering prosecution of terrorism.
   D. All the above.

DISCUSSION EXERCISES

1. Why are most terrorism prosecutions conducted under federal law?

2. What are the arguments as to why or why not Terrorism should be a state crime, as well as a federal crime?

3. What free speech concerns might be raised by Penal Law Article 490?

4. Could a Terrorism prosecution under Article 490 result in the prosecution of people not generally considered terrorists? For example, could a farmer who loses his farm through a foreclosure be guilty of terrorism if he threatens to drive his tractor through the county courthouse to oppose what he calls the "anti-people" judge who ordered the sheriff to take the farmer's farm?

5. What, if anything, does a statute prohibiting terrorism offer that traditional penal statutes did not?

Chapter 14

Answers to Multiple Choice Questions

Chapter One
1. c
2. b
3. d
4. b
5. b
6. a
7. d
8. a
9. b
10. b
11. d
12. b
13. b
14. b
15. b
16. b
17. c
18. c
19. d
20. a
21. b

Chapter Two
1. c
2. b
3. c
4. d
5. a
6. d
7. b
8. d
9. b
10. b
11. b

Chapter Three
1. d
2. b
3. b
4. d
5. b
6. c

Chapter Four
1. c
2. d
3. d
4. b
5. b

Chapter Five
1. a
2. a
3. b
4. b
5. b

Chapter Six
1. b
2. c
3. c
4. d
5. c
6. a

Chapter Seven
1. d
2. b
3. c
4. c
5. b

Chapter Eight
1. b
2. b
3. b
4. d
5. b
6. b
7. e
8. b